THE COMPLETE BOOK OF

GOLF PRACTICE

THE COMPLETE BOOK OF

GOLF PRACTICE

Vivien Saunders

Illustrated by Chris Perfect

Stanley Paul

London Melbourne Auckland Johannesburg

Stanley Paul & Co. Ltd

The Random House Group Limited supports The Forest Stewardship
Council® (FSC®), the leading international forest-certification organisation.
Our books carrying the FSC label are printed on FSC®-certified paper.
FSC is the only forest-certification scheme supported by the leading
environmental organisations, including Greenpeace. Our
paper procurement policy can be found at
www.randomhouse.co.uk/environment

First published 1988
© Vivien Saunders 1988

ISBN 9780091945091

Printed and bound in Great Britain by Clays Ltd, St Ives plc

Contents

Acknowledgements

The author and publishers would like to thank Phil Sheldon, Ken Lewis/Sports Photo-Graphics and Peter Dazeley for the use of their copyright photographs in this book.

Introduction

It is unlikely that any golfer has ever reached championship standard at the game without putting in hours of work on the practice ground. For some this practice is seen as an inevitable evil en route to success and is sheer hard work. For others the hours spent on the practice ground are as much pleasure – if not more – as the time spent playing the course. To some there is a therapeutic fascination in hitting golf balls at a major tournament as dusk gathers over the practice ground with the poor unfortunate caddie peering increasingly helplessly into the gloom to trace the flight of any slightly stray shot. There seems to be a certain pride at hitting the last shot of the day before nightfall and a security in knowing that every last opportunity to perfect the technique has been grasped. Perhaps there is a kind of satisfaction in hearing the irreverent mumblings of the last spectator to leave the practice ground, implying some form of insanity in the player's perseverance, while having to admit defeat for his own staying power. Whatever the reason, to them practice is an obsession – the search for an impossible degree of perfection.

For the top-class golfer practice serves many purposes. There are times when there is some niggling little problem of technique which may cause a less than perfect flight to the ball. Practice is then a mission of fault finding and working painfully slowly to find the thought which produces the necessary correction for the next day or week. At other times practice may involve learning and developing some completely new little piece of theory to tighten up the swing. There is then the continuous process of keeping the swing finely tuned in much the same way as the sports-car enthusiast is always tinkering with this and that to keep the engine running at optimum performance. For a day or period of a few days the ball may be tending to the right, the next to the left. In between is that illusive point of perfection. Then again there is the form of practising or loosening up which is part of the daily ritual of tournament play, when the professional is experimenting and familiarizing himself with the swing he has woken with that morning. One day the set-up and swing may feel absolutely comfortable; the next, without any perceivable difference, just that tiny bit awkward. The player tries to find the feeling of comfort or comes to terms with the little imperfection. But then lastly there is the form of practice which the club golfer so rarely uses – the grooving of technique during a period when everything is at its best. The swing may feel good, the set-up comfortable and the ball flies along its desired path. Now is the time when the good player can work at his game, building up the feeling of the good swing, storing in his subconscious the sensation of the right movements. Club golfers tend to look upon practice as something which is worthwhile when things go wrong. They see it as a necessity only in times of trouble. The champion perhaps works harder and longer when things are going well, forming good habits and building confidence.

There are then many kinds of practice – learning afresh, fault finding, loosening up, strengthening, grooving the technique and practising to cope with the rigours and pressures of tournament play. Some players achieve a great deal from their practice by carefully planning each session, monitoring the results and keeping fairly meticulous records. Others put in hours of time without real success. Sometimes it is perhaps because of insufficient understanding of the mechanics of the swing, sometimes more a case of practising with little objective and failing to relate practice to what is necessary on the course. The player needs to work with a three-stage process in mind – learning to make his technique work on the practice ground, developing it to work in a playing situation, and finally grooving it as firmly as possible to withstand the pressures of a competitive situation.

The aim of this book is to give the player ideas of exercises and thoughts for correcting certain errors and improving all departments of the game, together with practice routines to make practice more interesting and beneficial. There are ideas for simulating the pressure of a playing situation, ideas for competitive practice routines in pairs or groups, exercises for loosening and strengthening the golfing muscles and ideas for monitoring progress on and off the course. The book is not only aimed at the player from 'rabbit' to champion but written also with the professional coach in mind, giving ideas which may be helpful in coaching both individuals and groups of every age and standard.

1 Fault Finding

I am sure that many golfers who spend long hours on the practice ground or driving range achieve far less than they should because of a sad lack of understanding of some of the most basic principles of golf. To many, the game is a mystery and remains so for the whole of their golfing life.

One of the most crucial pieces of basic information to understand about golf is that it is a game of spin and curves. The dimples on the ball are aerodynamically designed to encourage backspin. But in being able to take up backspin the ball is also very readily able to take up sidespin. It is this that sends the ball curving away to right or left so easily. In most ball games the skill of the good player is often one of being able to put spin on the ball to produce a curving flight. In golf it is just the reverse. The first stage for any golfer has to be to be able to hit the ball without imparting sidespin so that the ball flies in a straight line rather than veering off to right or left. Although most golfers appreciate that the golf ball bends, they often seem to lack understanding of why this happens and in many cases, although they see the ball curve away to right or left, make their adjustments to the swing as though the ball were flying straight out to the side, ignoring the element of spin.

For those who are natural games players of some other sport it is worth thinking of spin by comparison with another game. The tennis player of reasonable standard can probably feel the sensation of a cut shot, where the ball lands softly. The action is a cut-across shot. Much the same applies with a table-tennis bat, with a squash racket and so on. The feeling of these shots is much the same as a slice. At the opposite end of the range of shots is the tennis player's top spin, forehand drive, which equates very largely to the more correct feeling of hitting a golf ball, and is rather more like the hooked or drawn shot. In each case sidespin is put on the ball.

In golf, spin is imparted if the clubface at the moment of impact is not looking in the same direction as the direction of the swing itself. If the clubface is 'open' to this line of swing it produces a glancing blow and a cutting, slicing action. If the clubface is 'closed', i.e. looking to the left of the line of swing, there is a tendency to put hookspin on the ball. It is the grip and working of the hands and wrists that largely control this. We will see later the ways in which the grip can be adjusted and ideas for practising the different types of actions to eliminate hook and slice.

The danger for the club golfer is that he may well look at a faulty flight to his shots and try to ignore the element of spin. If he sees the ball veering away to the right, with a slice, he probably instinctively tries to correct the shot as though the ball were flying straight out to the right. Instead of working at a change in the feeling of his grip or hand action he is likely to try to steer the ball more to the left, producing a more pronounced cut-across action than he started with. The problem worsens and his corrections may be doing more and more harm. He forgets the element of spin. He may not understand it.

Looking at the Flight

In trying to make corrections to any shot, it is first of all necessary to look at the flight of the ball and to think quite carefully what is happening. If the flight is virtually at random, the golfer should simply hit more shots until a pattern of errors is produced. It is simply inconsistency. But once there is obviously a pattern to the shots, this should begin to tell the player his likely faults. The need is to look at the flight and to think of two particular elements to direction. Where did it start? How did it curve? A ball which starts comparatively straight and then swerves away to the right is by no means the same as one which pushes straight out to the right with no curve. The club player often tries to correct them in the same way without appreciating the difference. Where did it start? How did it spin?

In general terms a ball will start in the direction of the swing at the moment of impact. If the ball starts right of impact then the odds are that, providing it is hit from the middle of the clubface, the direction of the swing was right aimed through impact. This may be a question of aiming offline or of producing a faulty direction to the attack on the ball. If on the other hand the ball curves to the right, this is produced by the clubface being open at impact,

Table 1 A Perfect Contact

Basic principle

The ball needs to be struck from the approximate centre of the clubface to propel it forward. The clubhead needs to brush or otherwise make contact with the exact spot on which the ball sits for the loft of the club to take effect. The contact needs to be accurate and this is more a question of developing a good eye than absolute precision in the swing.

Shots from the toe

The swing comes down too near the feet as a result of:

1. standing too far from the ball
2. pulling in through impact.

Shots from the heel/socket

The swing comes down too far from the feet as a result of:

1. falling towards the ball by impact
2. swinging the shaft rather than thinking of the clubhead
3. standing too far from the ball and falling towards it
4. standing too close (not as common as players imagine).

Topped shots

The player hits the top of the ball as a result of:

1. looking at the top of the ball instead of the back of it
2. bad depth judgement through lack of experience
3. pulling in and up through impact
4. trying to lift the ball and so lifting the clubhead by impact.

Fat shots

The player hits behind the ball as a result of:

1. having the ball too far forward, i.e. left in the stance
2. producing too steep an attack
3. loosening the club at the top of the backswing
4. falling back on the right foot by impact.

General inconsistency

The player may start the ball almost at random from toe, heel, thin or fat. This is usually through lack of experience and not having developed a good eye for the size of the ball, aggravated by any tendency not to watch the ball through impact.

Table 2 The Correct Angle of Attack

Basic principle

The ball needs to be struck slightly on the upswing for a driver, at the bottom of the swing for the fairway woods and slightly on the down-swing for the irons. The shorter the iron and the worse the lie, the steeper the attack. The better the lie and longer the club, the shallower the attack can be.

Too steep an attack

An attack which is too steep on the ball tends to produce skied drives and excessive height into the wind. A steep attack tends towards being an attack from 'out to in' and is frequently linked to cut shots and slicing. It is perhaps the commonest problem of the club golfer. The causes can be:

1. excessive bending over at address
2. holding the head too low (particularly spec-tacle-wearers)
3. a steep shoulder tilt rather than turn
4. lifting the club and taking it straight back instead of inside
5. having the ball too far back, i.e. right at address
6. swaying to the left through impact.

A shallow attack

A shallow attack is generally produced from a swing in which the club is taken back on the inside and attacked from the inside. The estab-lished player is unlikely to be troubled by too shallow an attack. For a beginner it is linked to trying to lift the ball. Too shallow an attack is unlikely unless:

1. the player tries to lift the ball with the club-head rising
2. the player falls back and tries to lift the ball
3. the player lacks a steep attack for bad and downhill lies.

Table 3 Starting the Ball On-Target

Basic principle

A ball hit from near the centre of the clubface tends to start in the direction of the swing at impact.

Ball starts left of target

The ball is attacked with a left-aimed, out-to-in swing as a result of:

1. aiming left
2. open, i.e. left-aimed, shoulders producing insufficient turn
3. insufficient backswing turn
4. the ball too far forward at address
5. right-side dominance from the top of the backswing.

Ball starts right of target

The ball is attacked in an in-to-out, right-aimed direction as a result of:

1. aiming right
2. the ball too far back in the stance
3. swaying ahead of the ball through impact
4. insufficient turn through with a blocked leg action
5. having an exaggerated in-to-out idea.

General inconsistency

The ball may start to right and left almost at random. Look to the following causes:

1. lack of target awareness – no mental picture of the target
2. standing too far from the ball
3. inconsistent routine in aiming.

i.e. facing away to the right. The first requires a change to the set-up or the attack on the ball, while the second may require a change to the grip, or certainly a change to the hand action, through and before impact.

There are, however, other elements to the flight of the ball which need consideration and should give you a guide to the likely errors in the swing and contact with the ball. The five factors we are aiming for are as follows:

1. A perfect contact
2. The correct angle of attack
3. Starting the ball on target
4. Eliminating sidespin
5. Producing clubhead speed.

Look at any pattern of faulty shots in terms of these five factors.

Tables 1 to 5 show the basic principles which in the main govern each of these factors and the likely causes of faults which arise.

Table 4 Eliminating Sidespin

Basic principle

The ball flies in a straight line if and only if the clubface is square, i.e. facing in the same direction as the direction of swing at impact. The less loft on the club, the more pronounced the spin. An open clubface spins the ball with cut spin to the right and a closed one with hook spin to the left.

Ball curves to the left

The clubface is closed through impact in relation to the line of the swing as a result of:

1. the left hand being too much on top of the grip, and/or
2. the right hand too much under in the grip
3. the wrists roll and close the clubface through impact with a flat, round-the-body finish
4. the clubface shuts in the backswing, i.e. looking down in the takeaway and up at the top of the backswing
5. the player is very right-hand dominant through impact
6. (unusual) the player has an in-to-out swing with the clubface on target.

Ball curves to the right

The clubface is open through impact with the player imparting cutspin – a cut-across action – as a result of:

1. the left hand is insufficiently on top of the club and/or
2. the right hand is insufficiently underneath in the grip
3. the clubface is open at address
4. the clubface opens in the backswing, toe down at the top
5. the pivot is insufficient and the player cuts across the shot
6. hand action is slow and lifeless
7. grip pressure is too tight and the wrists immobilized.

Table 5 Producing Clubhead Speed

Basic principle

Distance is produced by clubhead speed (combined with its weight). Clubhead speed is, for all but the world-class golfer, produced by looseness and freedom rather than a feeling of strength and aggression. Looser equals faster.

Poor clubhead speed

This tends to arise from:

1. fear and lack of freedom
2. tension
3. too tight a grip, both fingers and wrists
4. left arm blocking and firm rather than turning and folding
5. a slicer's grip
6. bad timing
7. slowing down with a short, stunted finish.

The set-up from in front with a medium iron. The
set-up prepares the player for his swing. The feet
should be shoulder width, setting the weight
towards the insides of the feet, knees knocked in
slightly to encourage correct leg action, and with the
right foot virtually straight ahead, left foot out a
little to encourage the right degree of turn. The
right hand being below the left, the right shoulder
must be allowed to drop below the left, left arm
relaxed but straight, right one relaxed and slightly
tucked in (photo: Jack Nicklaus)

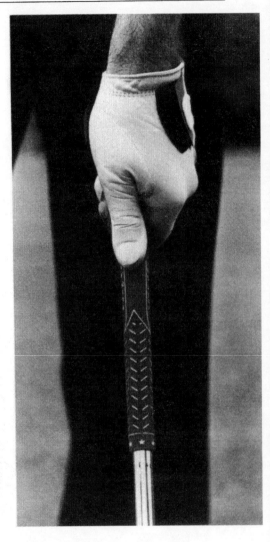

The grip from beneath. In the Vardon grip the fingers have to take up a particular spread. The little finger has to be separated from the others to fit round the index finger of the left hand; the index finger needs to be separated to produce a powerful trigger effect. The last two fingers of the left hand squeeze hard for maximum control (photo: Seve Ballesteros)

The grip from front. A good grip is aimed at returning the clubface squarely to the ball. It is formed with a feeling of pointing the fingers almost along the shaft, rather than straight round it. The hands are predominantly to the side of the club, but with the left if anything slightly on the top and the club resting in the fingers of the right. The right index finger should be spread a little away from the second finger, into a fairly powerful 'trigger' position, with the tip of the right thumb balancing this to the left of the shaft. The exact positioning of the hands is crucial in returning the clubface squarely at impact, and this is largely controlled by the direction of the Vs between thumb and index finger of each hand. The further either or both of

these Vs point towards the right shoulder (or even outside it) the more likely the player is to hook and less likely to slice. The nearer the Vs point to the chin (or even left of it) the more likely he is to slice

The set-up from behind the line of the shot. The posture at address should see the player essentially standing tall, bending from the top of the legs, by sticking the bottom out and up, from there relaxing or slightly flexing the legs according to height, without any pronounced drooping in the back. With the bottom out and back the hands can be beneath the chin, the wrists slightly cupped, arms hanging close to the body, so that the player has a feeling of standing relatively near to the ball rather than stretching away from it. The direction of the body, from feet to shoulders, is set parallel to the line of flight in a square stance, resisting any tendency for the right hand to pull the right shoulder forward instead of down (photo: Bernhard Langer)

2 Long Game Exercises

The Grip

Hand separation

In forming a good grip the right hand needs to take up a particular spread, with the little finger and index finger stretched away from the other two. The little finger hooks around and between the first and second fingers of the left; the right index finger needs to be slightly extended into a triggering position. This spread is often difficult to produce, with a tendency to bunch the fingers of the right hand together, causing a clumsy, insensitive grip. As an exercise simply practise spreading the hand, opening and closing the fingers, and then feel this spread in forming the grip.

Gripping for comfort

The inexperienced golfer often finds difficulty in gripping the club comfortably and yet reasonably quickly. With tennis and other ball games you usually have the racket, stick, bat or whatever in your hands virtually continuously throughout the game. In golf you not only have a whole set of clubs to master, but have to be able to decide which club to use and then take it out of the bag, make friends with it quickly and feel comfortable and ready to hit within a matter of seconds. For the club golfer this feeling of discomfort with the grip is often the difference between his performance on the range and the course. In practice he gains comfort; in play he has to take out the club afresh. An ideal exercise for the long-handicap

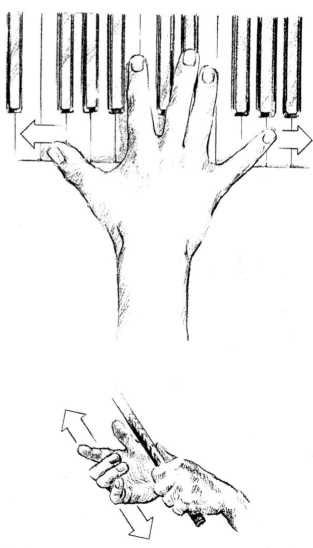

Hand separation for forming the Vardon grip

player is to keep a club at home and practise forming the grip quickly and easily. Left hand, right hand and feel comfortable immediately. Keep repeating, twenty grips at a time, checking the appearance from time to time in a mirror, until the hands go on in two movements. If the grip is really good the player should be able to pick up the club, eyes closed, and still get the hands on correctly. The shape of the grip – which isn't completely round – and balance of the clubhead give the hands the feeling for getting the clubface square.

Gripping afresh

The club golfer needs to practise forming the grip. In a lesson or practice session the hands should be set afresh for each shot. The pupil often expects the professional to set up the ball for him and then keep the hands firmly on the club shot after shot. This is invariably a sign of awkwardness in setting the hands. In practice, the long-handicap player often sets the grip and pulls ball after ball towards himself to hit, again without regripping. The player obviously feels unhappy in forming the grip and this often explains why his performance in practice is better than in play.

Avoiding the 'piccolo' grip

Players who are not particularly strong in the hands often tend to let go of the club at the top of the backswing. Sometimes the right hand opens off the left thumb. More commonly the last two fingers of the left hand loosen and lose control. The fault in flight is usually one of fat shots – hitting behind the ball. A good exercise, as well as strengthening the fingers of the left hand, is to put a tee peg or matchstick between the very end of the club and the heel of the left hand, trying to retain this in the hand throughout the swing. Practising squeezing the last two fingers of the left hand to the palm of the hand will strengthen the grip.

Correcting a shifting grip

A common fault is to allow the hands to shift

before the start of the backswing or in the takeaway. Club golfer and professional alike often start to fidget with the hands, a problem which tends to be accentuated under pressure on the course. Starting the takeaway needs some definite movement to bring everything into action. Often either or both hands are wrongly allowed to turn on the club as the grip loosens or tightens. This needs to be carefully monitored and stopped. The watchful eye of a golfing companion and saying 'Stop' when the fidgeting starts is one cure. Another is to set up a row of four balls, six or so inches apart, starting to hit from one end of the row and working to the other without allowing the hands to move on the club. If the grip remains constant, the last shot will feel as comfortable as the first. If the grip slips, hitting all four without an adjustment is virtually impossible. Repeat the exercise until the hands stay in place. At first the hands may have to hold quite tightly to achieve this consistency. For good golfers and those with any tendency to slice, gradually try to achieve the same but with a lighter and more sensitive grip. It is also an ideal exercise for practising watching the ball well through impact.

The Set-up

Aiming over a spot

Aiming incorrectly can cause all kinds of directional problems. Ideally the player should see a straight line from the ball to the hole and stand parallel to this, with the entire body from feet to shoulders and the line of the eyes, set on the parallel line. This straight line is often hard to judge when viewed from the side of the ball.

The best way of aiming reliably is to get used to setting the club to the right of the ball, walking behind it and looking at the shot along the line rather than from the left of the ball. Stand about three or four feet behind the ball and look at the target, choosing a spot on the ground about 15 to 18 inches ahead of the ball and on line with your target. Now walk round to address the ball, keeping this spot firmly in

Stopping a fidgeting grip with the help of a golfing friend

mind. Set the clubface square to this line rather than to the flag in the distance, stand with your feet together at right angles to this imaginary line from ball to spot, place the feet apart systematically, left foot first, then the right, and adopt the parallel line. Then trust yourself to hit out over this spot. If you look up at the target again, resist any temptation to move the feet or to realign the shoulders. Practise choosing the spot and your lining-up routine until it becomes second nature.

Practising alignment

At the first sign of any directional problems with your shots, check the alignment of your feet. Set a club down along your toes and view this from behind. The club should not point at your target but *parallel to* the proposed line of flight. If you check this before hitting the ball it is easy to see the line you hope the ball would fly on. If checking after the ball has gone it is worth setting another club down to form the

parallel line. As part of your practice routine aim to different targets and check your alignment with a club. Either hit the ball to your various targets and monitor the results, or simply see it as an exercise to practise aiming – an exercise you can easily use in the fairly confined space of a garden. On the practice ground choose five different targets and hit to these at random, making your aiming routine crucial and simulating the novelty of each shot in a round.

Monitoring the ball position

The ideal ball position varies from one player to another. As a guideline the stronger and better a player, the further to the left he is likely to be able to play the ball. Older players and most women need to play the ball further back. The ball is played furthest to the left with a driver to encourage an upward, sweeping attack, and further to the right in the stance, the shorter the club and worse the lie, to encourage a more downward attack. Having decided on the ideal ball position it is by no means easy to keep it consistent. Good golfers have more problems arising from the set-up and in particular the ball position than from almost anything else. It is difficult to look down at your own ball position and judge it accurately.

One of the best ways to check the ball position is to set one clubshaft down along your toes and the other at right angles across this towards the ball to see the precise position of the ball in relation to the feet. The results are often quite different from what the player imagines. This may immediately indicate if there is an error – for the club golfer more often than not that the ball is too far forward, i.e. to the left.

But frequently it is hard to find a comfortable position and the feeling one week may be quite different the next. An ideal way of monitoring the ball position is to check it when things are going well and to keep a definite record of the position. When the feeling is good, stand on a large sheet of newspaper or wallpaper, marking the spot where the ball would be and your foot position. Label the paper with the club used and put it away for future reference in times of difficulty.

Distance from the ball – precise measuring

As a simple guideline, the closer you can stand to the ball the better. Good players are unlikely to stand too close for long without feeling uncomfortable. High-handicap players can stand in close providing they adopt the correct posture, sticking the bottom out to get the body out of the way. But it is all too common to stand too far from the ball, good players often coming to grief by stretching further from the ball when things are going well and just edging too far away for safety. Like the ball position, distance from the ball needs constant reviewing and is hard to check oneself. The newspaper exercise above is ideal for this too.

The good golfer needs to aim for precision and I would suggest should measure and record distance from the ball with a tape measure or ruler during a spell of playing well, using the

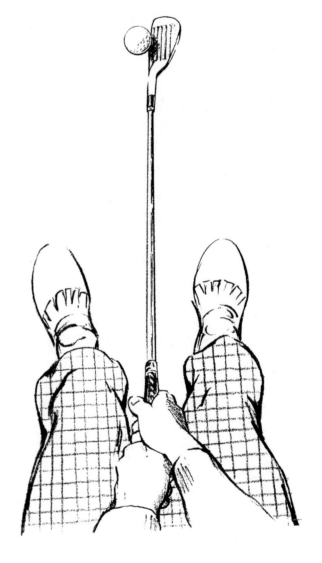

Above Recognizing the correct distance and ball position from your view of it

Right Bottom up and out – *not* sitting and sagging at address driver and 5-iron for reference. An error of an odd inch can throw out the arc of the club through impact to the point where direction becomes erratic. Another way of measuring the exact distance is to set the club on the ground from the ball to the line of your feet, end of the hosel by the ball, and to mark with tape or waterproof ink the distance of your toes from the ball. It is, of course, a reference which must not be used in actual play.

Distance from the ball – visual guide

In play you need to keep your distance from the ball as constant as possible without being able to take precise measurements. This has to be a question of feel. The distance of the right elbow from the body can act as a guide. The feeling of balance on the feet can be another. One way in which you can assess the distance and encourage a consistent set-up is to look at the position of your hands in relation to the

chin. With the ball in fairly close, the hands should feel to be under the chin rather than under the forehead. But what you will also see is the visual relationship of your hands to your toes. If standing in you may feel that your right index finger appears roughly level with the feet; you may feel the hands always appear outside the line of the feet. Make a mental or written note of the appearance of this relationship, again while playing well, for future reference.

Perfecting posture

The posture in the set-up tends to dictate the plane of swing, the way in which arms and body move in the backswing and the use of the legs in the throughswing. Club golfers, advised to adopt a position like one of sitting on a shooting stick, tend to sag at the knees and consequently droop in the back into a stance which lacks power. The correct feeling in the set-up should be one of standing up tall, pushing the hips back and up as though lifted from the back

trouser pockets, and only with the bottom out and up in this way to flex the knees. With the bottom sticking out the arms are able to hang loosely, hands below the chin, wrists dropped slightly.

An excellent way of checking and improving the posture is to stand with the heels about four inches from a wall, pushing the bottom out and up to touch the wall as high as possible. From there, slide the bottom a couple of inches down the wall as the knees flex. This is quite different from the wrong, sagging posture, where the player could stand with the heels against the wall and just slide down it into a powerless position.

Relaxation at address

There should be a feeling of relaxation at address, particularly in the arms and shoulders. The correct feeling should be of the arms hanging loosely downward to the sides of the body, shoulders down – almost forced down – rather than the shoulders coming up and forward with the arms out from the body as though over the chest. To produce the correct feeling in the arms and shoulders, stand up erect and have the feeling from a tall position of forcing the shoulders down, not forward, trying to stretch the arms down to have the hands as low as possible to your sides. Compare this in a mirror with the incorrect feeling of the shoulders lifting, where tension would show, collarbone rising. In this way the hands can seem to be held low at address without any feeling of slouching in the back and shoulders, and the posture encourages a good grip, fingers almost along the club. With the arms hanging to the side, bend from the top of the legs until the hands can be brought together under the chin with the arms still feeling loose.

The right shoulder position

One of the hardest parts of the set-up for the club golfer is to have the feeling of comfort with

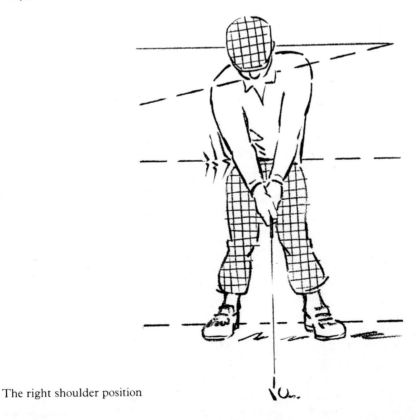

The right shoulder position

the right shoulder below the left. The right hand is below the left on the club. One of two things follow from this. Either the right hand tends to pull the right shoulder forward – this is wrong – or the right shoulder drops neatly below the left – this is correct. Achieving this isn't always easy. It is not a question of having the weight on the right foot, nor of feeling that the left hip is pushed out, body arching sideways. It should simply be a feeling of compressing the right side of the body from hip to shoulder and if anything stretching the left. Men with a long back tend to find this easy while women with shorter backs or people with stiffness in the back often find it unnatural. It is an essential part of the set-up. Without it there is a tendency for the right shoulder to ride too high, encouraging a steep swing and aggravating any likelihood of slicing. A very simple loosening exercise is to stand erect, feet apart, sliding the right hand down the right leg without tipping the hips. Right side compresses, left side stretches. Having produced this feeling, bend from the hips to feel it in relation to the address position.

Squareness of the shoulders

It is often hard to keep the shoulders feeling square and comfortable. For many players the right shoulder often feels dominant at address. This will frequently happen if the player is too far from the ball and/or the ball too far forward to the left. The easiest way of checking this is to practise with, say, a 5-iron, playing the ball in varying ball positions until the right shoulder feels square. The further back the ball is played, the easier this may feel.

The Backswing

Toe up for beginners

The feeling of the backswing for the average club golfer usually needs to be one of combining a turn of the left side of the body followed by a lifting of the arms. The first stage to this is to turn from the left shoulder, bringing the club back fairly low until roughly level with the legs. If the shoulders turn correctly and with a suitable grip, the toe of the club should be pointing virtually upwards, the club knee to hip high. From this position the hands and wrists can naturally hinge upwards to form a simple backswing. As a practice routine the beginner needs to practise this first stage, toe up and then hinging up with the wrists to a point where the thumbs, and in particular the left thumb, support the club at the top of the backswing, wrists cocked.

Perfecting the plane

In an ideal backswing the shoulders should turn, with the angle of the left arm above the plane of the shoulders. One of the most common errors for club golfers is to adopt too steep a plane with the shoulders, so that the left shoulder drops in the backswing. This tends to result in the right hand and arm being too dominant at the top of the backswing, encouraging an out-to-in attack and aggravating any tendency to slice the ball, sky drives and lose power generally. There are two ways of lifting the hands to the top of the backswing. One is to make the club rise by dropping the left shoulder; this is quite wrong. The other, which is correct, is to have the feeling of turning the shoulders and lifting the arms. One of the difficulties of golf is that the ball sits on the ground and the ground gets in the way. Many players' way round this is to lift the club unsuitably in the backswing to produce a feeling of getting down into it again.

In the wrong position the left shoulder drops and the player has the feeling of looking several inches beyond the shoulder down to the ball. In the correct position the shoulder turns rather than lifts, and the ball will appear only just visible above the shoulder as you view it from the top of the backswing. The *feeling* will almost be that the left shoulder lifts rather than drops – in fact it stays virtually level – and that the club is lifted by the left arm and not forced up by the shoulder dropping. The left shoulder covers the chin (and almost the mouth); never let the

The correct plane of swing, and the incorrect steep plane which frequently causes a slice

chin protrude above the shoulder.

To produce the correct feeling repeat the backswing, twenty swings in succession, feeling a two-piece action of turning the left shoulder and lifting the left arm, feeling the left shoulder covering the chin and ensuring that the ball is only just visible above the shoulder. If you overdo it you will lose sight of the ball. The exercise is generally easier the longer the club, for the extra length tends to encourage a flatter plane and discourage the steep one. Once the backswing begins to take shape, add the down and throughswing, first without the ball, swinging under the left shoulder but with no feeling of forcing the right shoulder down.

The right arm

In the correct plane of backswing the right arm should fold away to form a virtual right angle, elbow pointing down. A good, old-fashioned exercise is to practise swinging to the top of the backswing with a golf ball lodged under the right armpit. This necessitates keeping the right arm folding in and not flapping out. It is perhaps slightly exaggerated in producing a rather cramped swing if followed too religiously, but is good for encouraging the correct feel to the plane.

Carrying a tray

Another way of feeling the correct right hand and arm position at the top of the backswing is to adopt a position like a waiter carrying a tray. This again sees the elbow forming a right angle, right wrist folded back on itself.

Left-arm dominance

Ideally the backswing should feel dominated by the left side. The left shoulder makes the turn rather than the right. One would think turning the left shoulder or right shoulder would produce the same effect but they do not. With the left shoulder in control of the turn the shoulders stay rounded in together. With the right shoulder making the turn the shoulders and chest open and the right elbow may fly out from the body. Practising left-arm control is one of the finest exercises. As a starting point repeat the backswing twenty times, feeling the left arm to be in control, taking the right hand off the club at the top of the swing to feel the left thumb in a supporting role under the shaft of the club.

Once the left thumb feels as if it is supporting the club, practise the backswing with the left hand only, starting from a stationary position at address, lifting it smoothly away to a firm, controlled backswing. Pause for a moment and then return smoothly to a stationary set-up.

Left-arm strengthening

To strengthen the left arm, swing the club to the top of the backswing, left arm only. Now bounce the club up and down 10 to 12 inches, feeling the arm and hand fully in control.

The left wrist

Once at the top of the backswing with the left arm only, practise hinging the wrist over and back, building this up to twenty or thirty twists. This gradually builds up the left wrist, helping to produce the flattish left wrist which usually accompanies a good backswing.

Feeling the right arm and hand backswing position

The left arm position

Ideally the left arm should stay straight in the backswing. This gives a degree of extension and encourages a repetitive position. Some golfers find it almost impossible to keep the arm straight. The correct feeling of a really tightly coiled backswing should be one of drawing the left arm across the chest towards the right shoulder, the arm always at a slightly higher angle than the plane of the shoulders. In a perfectly orthodox backswing position the left arm is drawn close to the right shoulder. The club golfer often tries to achieve this without being

physically able to, either because of tightness in the back of the left arm and shoulder or through a heavily built upper chest. To produce the correct feeling in the left arm and develop looseness, hold the left arm straight out in front, palm down, put the right hand behind the left elbow and ease the arm across the chest towards the shoulder. The player who keeps a good, straight left arm in the backswing will generally be able to ease the arm to the right shoulder, keeping it perfectly straight. The player who feels the movement restricted in the exercise

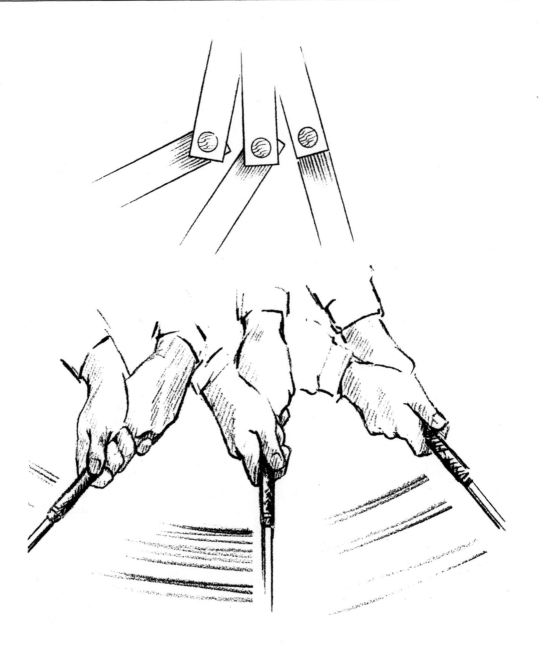

Feeling the correct backward hinging of the wrists

will need to make allowances in the golf swing, either coming to terms with an arm that bends, or having to turn the shoulders more to get the left arm into a suitable position for the downswing. Practising the movement without a club, right hand assisting to ease it across, will gradually loosen the back of the left upper arm. Moving the arm unaided from fully left to fully right and towards the right shoulder will encourage the feeling of the left arm movement in the swing. Bend into a semi-address position, without a club, and move the left arm alone from in front to the right shoulder, letting the palm of the hand turn to simulate the backswing.

Developing the wrist action

For the fairly advanced player the wrist cock is no longer an upward hinging of the wrists. Instead the right wrist should hinge back on itself in the tray-carrying position. To encourage this correct wrist cock, build in a couple of backward waggles before the takeaway, hinging the right wrist back on itself, arms staying virtually motionless. The club should travel back in a low, shallow curve in this waggle. Practise this backward hinging as a separate exercise, loose wrists, to encourage the correct inside takeaway. The correct takeaway, following a waggle, in turn encourages an attack from the inside, with the club coming from behind the player and *not* straight down the line of the shot.

Avoiding an overswing

Women golfers in particular are often worried by an overswing, the club shaft being well beyond the horizontal at the top of the backswing. This can happen through the player being extremely supple (which causes little problem) or from a loosening grip, a bending left arm or from a late wrist cock. Whatever the cause, the result is usually loss of power and a tendency to hit behind the ball. The club golfer will often overswing because of trying to copy the look of professional golfers and confusing appearance and feel. Professional golfers

usually seem to have a wide, stretched backswing, with the wrists seeming to cock at about hip or waist height. The player copies what he thinks happens and will often swing back to what feels like waist height before bringing the hands into play. The wrist cock then happens too late in the swing, with the arms above the head and the hands and wrists dropping unsuitably. What the professional golfer usually does is to feel that the hands are active right from the moment of the takeaway, wrists beginning to cock as the arms start their swing. The wrist cock shows rather later than it feels. (Any golfer told he cocks the wrists too soon probably fails to move the arms back as the wrists hinge – the arms moving late rather than the wrists too early.)

An exercise for shortening the swing is to practise with a 6 or 7-iron, cocking the wrists as early as possible on the backswing (and throughswing) to shorten the swing for a crisp, punchy shot. The player is usually surprised at the length and power achieved and can gradually adapt the feeling to the longer clubs.

Curing a locked right leg

In the backswing the shoulders, and to a lesser extent the hips, should turn to produce the correct direction to backswing and downswing. For players who need a fairly large hip turn, particularly women and older men, there is a danger of the right leg straightening and the knee locking back. This usually immobilizes the legs in the start of the downswing. To correct this it is first necessary to adopt the correct foot position at address. The feet need to be set with the outsides of the feet outside the width of the shoulders *and hips*. This means that the hip and leg turn is more easily contained within the width of the stance without any tendency to roll onto the outside of the right foot. The weight should be concentrated towards the inside of the right foot, feeling it pressing down on the inside of the foot, while transferring the weight correctly in the backswing. An exercise to encourage the correct feeling is to stand with a golf ball or clubshaft under the outside of the right foot at address,

Learning the contact by using a tennis ball

forcing the weight onto the inside of the foot. Turn and swing to the top of the backswing, feeling that weight transfers towards the right side in turning, but still feeling pressure on the inside of the foot. As a rule this feeling of staying on the inside of the foot combined with a turn stops the right leg locking and keeps the knee flexed in readiness for moving well through the ball by impact.

Contact Problems

Playing good golf requires a sound contact with the ball. It is perhaps the only ball game where the contact with the ball is difficult. The ball is small, the clubhead is small and the ball sits on the ground – the ground gets in the way. The long-handicap golfer often labours under the misapprehension that if the swing looks reasonably correct the club will strike the ball soundly. Sadly this just isn't so. Striking the ball from the middle of the club with the right depth of

contact requires a trained eye or very natural ball sense combined with an ability to watch the ball well to the moment of impact. This section of exercises is largely aimed at the beginner and long-handicap golfer, but with ideas for the experienced player who suffers occasional disastrous shots.

Learning the contact

The beginner often finds difficulty in transferring his practice swing to the ball because of its small size and the precision required. The general tendency is to try to lift the ball into the air, falling back on the right foot and in so doing catching the ground. An ideal way of learning, particularly for those who are not gifted games players, is to learn with a tennis ball or a light plastic ball that size. The extra size means that the player can more easily get the feeling of striking the ball below its centre, getting the ball to rise quite easily without any urge to scoop it up. Once the swing can be reasonably grooved with the larger ball, the next stage is to try with a smaller light ball or to progress to a golf ball, teeing it up on a low peg to instil confidence. The tee can then be lowered or removed altogether, at first sitting the ball on a tuft of grass to make the contact easier. This feeling for the depth of contact is very hard for many players and needs to be acquired systematically. If the player tries to hit a golf ball from bare ground as a beginner, he will usually find the contact so difficult that the swing itself is seen as being too complex and the natural swing can all too easily disappear. Using this exercise the player gradually improves the depth judgement without becoming obsessed with the swing.

Sweeping the fairway woods

The ideal contact with a fairway wood is to brush the ground on which the ball sits. Pro-

viding the whole ball sits above the ground, without settling in a depression, there is no need to strike it on the downswing. The sweeping contact produces good height and encourages maximum length. The depth of contact needs to be judged very finely, the barer the lie the more accurate the depth needs to be. It is important with these shots to produce practice swings where the sole of the clubhead brushes the ground – not just tickling the grass, but with the sole plate bouncing on the ground. On firm ground there should be a definite sound as the club bounces. One of the ways of practising this is to use a rubber driving-range mat, feeling the bouncing contact and gradually monitoring this until the contact is in precisely the right spot. The player will benefit from thinking of the sole plate on the bottom of the wood and of bouncing this onto the ground directly behind the ball, almost with a feeling of slapping it down behind the ball and drawing it up again

The bouncing/sweeping contact for a fairway wood

beyond impact. In learning to play good fairway woods, try initially from a very low tee, just setting the ball a fraction off the ground, and then reproduce the same feeling from increasingly bare lies, until good depth judgement is learned.

Watching the ball

The professional golfer can usually get away with looking away from the ball momentarily before impact, but will from time to time have to concentrate on watching it really well to produce a perfect strike. This is particularly the case from any bare or bad lie. The long-handicap player whose swing is less grooved certainly needs to look at the ball until the moment the ball is struck, being conscious of staying looking down and seeing the grass for a split second after the ball has gone, and yet completing the swing through to follow the flight of the ball. Many golfers find it almost impossible to stay with the ball long enough and have an irresistible urge to look up early. A way of practising the feeling of being able to watch the ball well is to hit a row of four balls, addressing each, hitting each and then looking at the next rather than following the flight of the previous one. The correct way of doing the exercise is to swing through to a full finish with each shot, holding it for a second or so before turning to the next, but still without following the flight. The player is gradually able to watch the ball well and complete the swing in an uninhibited way.

In watching the ball the eyes should focus on the back of the ball – the part the clubface is going to hit – rather than looking down at the ball as a whole or on its top. In practice or for the drive it is well worth setting the ball with the maker's name or number on the back to give some extra focal point, a coloured blob of ink acting as a definite reminder for players continually fighting the urge to look up too soon.

Checking the divot

Ideally in striking an iron shot the ball should be contacted slightly on the downswing, with the clubhead continuing through to take a divot. The divot should start as near as possible below the middle or front edge of the ball. Players who watch the ball well through impact are usually aware of their divots, knowing the feeling of crispness and perfect judgement. Longer-handicap players often mis-strike the ball by coming down too far behind the ball or too far ahead of it. Watching the divot and monitoring its precise position in relation to the ball can give feedback for making improvements. To assess the precise position of the divot and whether the contact is correct, put in a tee a couple of inches outside the middle of the ball. After hitting the ball, note the position of the back of the divot telling you quite simply whether there has been a tendency to hit the ball heavy or thin. The good golfer can feel the difference. The club golfer may not be aware of the exactness of the contact without this kind of proof.

Positioning on the clubface

It is essential to hit the ball from as near as possible to the middle of the clubface. Long-handicap players often produce an inconsistent contact, striking the ball almost at random from various parts of the clubface. Good players will usually produce a consistent strike but may find their shots creeping slightly towards toe or heel without necessarily knowing why the strike feels less than perfect. It is important to address the ball from the centre of the clubface. This sounds simple but isn't always straightforward. In looking down at the clubhead from the address there is frequently an optical illusion in that the ball viewed from this position and seeming to be central on the face is often further towards the heel than the player imagines. It is therefore worth checking the ball/clubface position from behind the club and ball. To make yourself aware of the centre of the face it is worth practising with a small piece of sticky paper (from the flap of an envelope for example) on the sweetspot of the clubface. But even with the ball addressed centrally on the clubface there is no guarantee that the strike will be perfect.

An exercise for checking the strike is to put a small blob of lipstick, chalk or coloured marker on the back of the ball, to strike it and then see where the telltale mark is left on the clubface. Long-handicap players may be surprised at the discrepancy in the results; top-class golfers can sometimes find themselves a fraction too near toe or heel for comfort. Having assessed the pattern of strike the long-handicap golfer will usually find improvement simply by repeating the exercise, perhaps hitting into a net, concentrating on the feeling and sound of connecting with the ball accurately and checking the feedback from the marks on the clubface. The low-handicap player will usually be able to rectify the errors simply by thinking in terms of the clubface contact, edging the ball back towards the sweetspot.

Curing a shank

One of the most devastating shots in golf is the shank or socket – the ball flying off the bottom of the shaft. Long-handicap players who produce

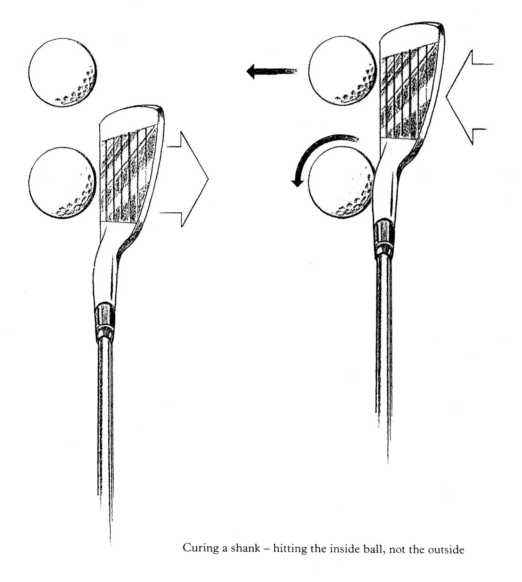

Curing a shank – hitting the inside ball, not the outside

these shots often do not know whether the ball has been struck from the end of the toe or from the socket. Both fly off to the right, of course, and although the feeling is quite different they are not necessarily able to distinguish one from the other. The first point is to be certain what the shot is. A simple way of checking the contact, and indeed to set about correcting it, is to address the ball with another ball or tee about an inch outside the target one. The player who sockets is likely to bring the club down too far from his feet and to catch both balls, often sending the outside one away more satisfactorily than the inside one. This feedback is often sufficient to enable him to cure the problem, concentrating on swinging the club through on the right path.

The socket is a common shot and once the player does a few it is a fault that tends to worsen. There are several reasons for shanking, but looking at the contact initially often helps the player. The socket may simply arise because the player swings the clubshaft, which is in effect an extension of the arms, rather than appreciating that the clubhead is extended out from this. The player may need to think hard of striking the ball from towards the toe, and even practise setting up to the ball and then deliberately swinging down and missing it on the inside to find judgement and control of the path the clubhead takes. Commonly players socket because of bad balance through impact, falling forward onto the balls of both feet through impact and so bringing the club down too far from the feet. The fault, indeed, is often one of standing too far from the ball and toppling forward slightly rather than, as the player usually assumes, standing in too close. This kind of socket can be cured most easily from a combination of good balance in the finish, emphasis being on the left heel through impact, and working on the two-ball exercise set out above.

Players who socket the ball from bad balance are often prone to hitting wood shots from the heel of the club, with the odd disaster which flies straight left. Again the beginner doesn't necessarily understand why the irons shoot off to the right and the woods to the left.

Shots from the toe

Hitting the ball from the toe is less common than the socket, but if the ball comes off the very end of the club it can be just as devastating. A good exercise for trying to correct shots from the toe is to place a tee peg a quarter of an inch or so outside the ball, with the idea that if the ball is struck from the middle of the club, the tee peg will be collected too. By careful positioning of the tee it is easy to get good feedback of what is happening through impact. Players who do hit the ball from the toe, and indeed those who tend to socket, produce these errors in practice swings as well as with the ball. Often they will exclaim 'I can do it without the ball' and yet the odd inch error through impact shows clearly. The fault is often closely allied to topping the ball, with a tendency to pull the arms in and up through impact instead of stretching and extending.

The upward driver contact

Hitting a teed-up ball with a driver requires a different contact from the fairway woods and irons. The ball, because it sits above the ground, can be struck on the upswing, giving maximum chance to produce clubhead speed and a penetrating trajectory. To help produce this upward contact, the ball is positioned well forward in the feet, perhaps an inch or so inside the left heel. The feeling, however, must be of keeping the weight fairly central in the feet and so behind the ball.

Players often have considerable difficulty in producing an upward contact with a driver, having mastered the downward or sweeping contact with the other clubs. Frequently there is a tendency to play the ball forward but then to sway to the left through impact, imparting a downward blow onto the ball. This tends to lead to striking it from the top of the clubhead, so that the ball takes off with excessive height. The correct feeling should be that the bottom of the swing skims the ground several inches behind the ball, roughly in line with the player's nose, and then moves on upward to collect the ball. With active footwork and a turn on through of the body there should be a definite sensation of rather more weight remaining on the tips of the toes of the right foot than with the other clubs.

To practise the correct contact with the driver, set up addressing an imaginary ball, having a feeling of sitting slightly towards the right foot. Concentrate on practice swings where the club very definitely brushes the ground, with a sensation of bouncing upwards a little, the contact being a good eight inches behind your imaginary ball. This should give you the feeling of the correct weight distribution. With the ball it should be much the same except that the clubhead should skim the ground rather than actually bouncing on it.

Other driving exercises

As a second exercise practise with the ball, tee it up in the correct place well forward in the feet, but with your clubhead initially set opposite the middle of your stance and so several inches behind the ball. Then edge the clubhead forward to the ball, feeling that the right shoulder drops under in so doing rather than coming round. Experiment with adopting the set-up in this way and experiment also at starting with the clubhead several inches behind the ball, and even looking a little behind the ball until the more upward strike can be appreciated.

The good player who finds trouble from time to time with the driver contact, perhaps producing the odd skied shot, can usually work through the problem if it arises during play by simply teeing the ball a little lower. But to correct the fault in practice an excellent exercise is to tee the ball particularly high. This means that the ball can only be solidly hit with the player staying behind the ball correctly with a definite feeling of having to hit up on the ball. Most good golfers find that the longest and best driving occurs with a feeling of being comfortable from a ball teed high. It usually means the body is set well behind the ball at address and through impact, with more time to accelerate the clubhead into the ball.

Monitoring direction

Many players who hit the ball offline simply don't start it out on target. There is often no real reason for this other than a poor sense of direction. To check this, preferably on a driving-range mat, position a coin or tee peg about 18 inches ahead of the ball directly on line with the target. Get someone to sit or squat behind the line of the shot to check whether the ball starts off on line. Good players if anything tend to start the ball right; club golfers more inclined to the left should check Table 3 for the reasons and likely corrections.

Fullswing Exercises

The inside attack

Most club golfers tend to hit the ball from out to in, i.e. with a left-aimed attack. This tends to arise from taking the club back on an outside or straight path, rather than swinging it back on the inside, and goes hand in hand with a steep backswing and attack and sliced shots. The path which the clubhead should describe is a curve, with no straight lines into or away from impact. The clubhead should travel back on an inside curve and attack the ball on a curve, with the ball flying off at a tangent to this curve on target. The smoother the curve as a rule the better, but never with any feeling of swinging the clubhead back on a straight line or through on a straight line. Swinging the club is much the same in principle as swinging a racket, where the racket head automatically moves round and behind the player going back and attacks the ball in a curve. To encourage this curved attack when practising on a driving range, mark the curved path with a piece of chalk, feeling that the clubhead travels back and through on it. To most club golfers it feels awkward to take the club back sufficiently on the inside. In attacking the ball on a curved path, the feeling may need to be one of hitting the ball with an exaggeratedly in-to-out attack, with the right elbow almost brushing the body before impact.

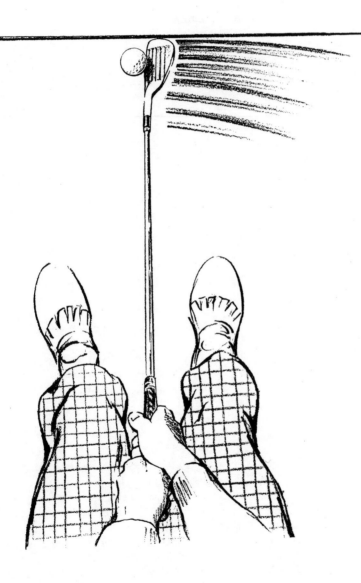

Hitting from the inside

Right Folding the left arm

Most players who slice the ball attack it with too steep a path, the clubhead coming slightly across the line of the shot from the outside. Low-handicap players often find it hard to believe the tendency to attack the ball from the outside and resist the idea of striking the ball in a more curved path. An exercise to encourage the correct path and to monitor precisely what happens, is to strike the ball with a light paper or plastic cup (or some similar object) positioned about 12 to 15 inches behind the ball and fractionally outside it. The best place to practise this is on a driving range when the ball can be set up uniformly on the mat. The edge of the cup nearest to you will need to be just outside the furthest side of the ball. This gives room for the toe of the club to miss it on the backswing and encourages the player to pass

inside it in the attack. Clearly an out-to-in attack will smash the cup en route to the ball. Once a player can see the path of the club he can usually begin to make the correction, combining the feeling of an inside attack with a shallower one. Conversely trying for a shallower attack will often encourage a more inside one. The player who slices will usually need to work at a combination of this feeling of an inside, curved attack with a loosening of the hands and wrists and turning both hands to the right on the club to square up or slightly close the clubface through impact.

Folding the left arm

In the backswing the left arm should stay straight to produce width and consistency. But

once the clubhead passes impact the left arm must start to turn and fold in precisely the same way as the right one did in the backswing. Ideally at address the left arm should hang so that the elbow bone points almost downwards towards the left hip rather than out towards the target. This is the way it is going to fold in the throughswing, folding neatly into the body and never staying stiff, and then breaking out towards the flag. Just beyond impact there is a point where both arms are flung out into an extended position. They are straight but in full shots not stiff. The left one must then start to turn and fold, elbow in, until the arm forms a nice, neat right angle at the end of the swing. There are several ways of practising this, one of which is to hold the club in the left hand grasping the inside of the elbow with the right hand. Swing the club through as though starting the throughswing, with very little backswing, and just feel the right hand pulling the left elbow in into a folding position. The left elbow should remain in front of you and visible out of the corner of the left eye. Precisely the same should happen in the swing. A left arm which stays too straight and stiff will usually result in the elbow moving out and behind you in the followthrough.

Understanding footwork

In the backswing the body turns. Weight is transferred round onto the ball of the left foot and heel of the right. The left heel may rise or it may stay down. What it must *not* do is to roll onto the inside of the foot. In the downswing weight is thrust back onto the left heel so that it is firmly on the ground through impact, the right foot spinning up on the toes. Always check the balance, feeling the weight on the left heel, so that the left toes are free and relaxed.

Leg action through the ball

By the end of the swing the hips and body should be turned through to face the target. To

Leg action through the ball – balance of left heel and right toes

achieve this the left heel must push firmly to the ground by impact, the right foot must spin up on the tips of the toes by the finish and the left leg must twist and straighten or virtually straighten to allow the hips through. The action of the left leg can prove difficult for many players. At address the left foot is turned out slightly, perhaps 20 degrees at the most. It stays in the same position through impact, meaning that the leg has to twist with the knee and hip facing the target. Often players have insufficient flexibility in the leg, with the result that it stays bent and leaves the hips facing right of target, usually resulting in shots pushed right or with unsuitable force from the shoulders. To practise this movement and loosen up the leg, stand with the feet apart, no club, and turn to the left, the leg twisting and straightening and the right foot spinning up on the toes. Having adopted this position, ease the hip and leg round, with a kind of bouncing action, until the movement begins to feel comfortable. The movement would of course be less important in the swing

with the left foot turned out more. The danger would be that this could inhibit the backswing turn.

Grooving the finish

Many golfers spend time trying to groove a backswing without appreciating the importance of a grooved finish. The club can only be accelerated through impact providing there is space for a free followthrough. Any action where the swing beyond the ball is inhibited usually results in loss of potential clubhead speed, the wrists frequently blocking the clubface open and tending to slice. Ideally at the end of a full drive the shaft of the club should settle against the player's left shoulder or back, with both arms folded and the hands somewhere beside the left ear. Frequently the problem is that the player swings the club too near his head, with an inhibited finish, saving himself from being hit on the top or back of the head. The need is to groove the finish until the club swings freely

Grooving the finish

clear of the head and rests on the shoulder.

The followthrough can be practised quite simply by adopting the address position and without any backswing turning to face the target, folding the arms to let the club hang loose on the left shoulder. As a first stage turn through and take the club roughly hip height, feeling the toe of the club pointing directly upwards. From there fold both arms, hands beside the left ear, club hanging loosely onto the shoulder with the elbows perhaps six inches or so apart, in approximate right angles and out in front of you. Keep repeating this movement, letting feet and legs turn through freely, until the swing is grooved and the club is always clear of the head. The feeling at the end of the swing should be of the chin being tucked in, never forced out by the right shoulder, and your view of the imaginary target would be with the right eye looking just past the right arm. Practise the throughswing until it is repetitive and then gradually add the backswing so that the two fall into place. With the ball aim for the same movements, emphasizing the feeling of the club-shaft – not the rubber grip – settling onto the left shoulder.

Practising with arms together

An excellent exercise for grooving the through-swing and for ensuring that the left elbow folds inwards instead of breaking out, is to practise with the elbows forced together. This also encourages a neat backswing position. Ideally use a piece of strong two- to three-inch elastic, sewn to form a loop or figure of eight, large enough to fit above both elbows. With the arms strapped together in this way, but with a little give in the elastic, the left arm is brought across to the right shoulder and the right elbow kept in on the backswing. In the followthrough the resistance of the elastic forces the left arm to begin to fold in instead of being allowed to break unsuitably outwards. It is perfectly possible to hit full shots up to the driver with this, and will often produce quite easily the feeling of the right movements.

The up-and-over finish

The ideal path of the clubhead attacking the ball is to strike the ball from 'inside', from there moving back inside but with a feeling of extension or swinging up the line of the shot. A common fault is to pull offline too soon after impact, with the result that with some shots the clubhead is offline by the moment of impact. To keep the club on target beyond impact you often need to allow the arms to fold so that the club swings out towards the target, up and over the left shoulder, without ever moving round and offline. The left arm needs to fold in and up rather than outwards. You should feel the body turning to face the target with the arms lifting and folding, and with the club travelling

Arms strapped together to encourage good direction through and beyond impact

almost (though not quite) straight back behind you in the followthrough. The more the elbows feel close together and in front of the left shoulder, the better the line will be.

To practise this a good exercise is to stand two feet or so from a wall at your back. Don't do the backswing for it would be quite wrong to be able to swing back without the wall getting in the way. But do try the feeling of the through-swing, turning the body through and slowly lifting and folding the arms so that they swing up and over and remain clear of the wall. The feeling will be of a turn through of the body and lift of the arms. In the swing at full speed the same kind of effect can be felt.

As a point of interest most club golfers could wrongly swing back with a wall behind them, as a result of lifting the club too steeply, but would then find the throughswing inhibited. The top-class player by contrast swings the club much more behind him in the backswing, and would hit the wall at perhaps knee height, but would then tend to swing through and up and over rather than round in the follow-through.

Training balance

Good balance in the golf swing is essential. The general tendency is to fall forwards towards the ball by impact, instead of having weight firmly on the left heel. Any player told that his swing is too fast is usually guilty of bad balance, making the swing look fast and untidy. An excellent exercise is to practise hitting full shots, holding the balance at the end of the follow-through for a count of four seconds. Club golfers often find this virtually impossible at first, feeling that the weight is beginning to fall forward. By holding the followthrough it means that the swing can be checked. Have the feet worked through correctly? Is the clubshaft resting neatly on the left shoulder? If there is any error it can be gradually corrected until it falls into place in the swing. Concentrating on balance usually means that the swing is kept smooth and unrushed. On the practice ground the aim should be to hold the finish for four seconds. By trying for the same effect on the course some sort of finish will usually be achieved, even if the player is suffering from tiredness or pressure towards the end of the round.

Kneeling to feel the plane

Many club golfers consistently swing with too steep a plane, encouraging a slice. A flatter plane encourages a draw. For the good golfer who wants to feel a flatter plane, an excellent exercise is to kneel down and hit the ball with a driver. Anything but a very flat plane tends to crash onto the ground many inches behind the ball. A flat plane can produce a shallow attack and will often give the player the feeling of a draw, which he can then transfer to his ordinary standing-up address position.

Flattening the plane

A good exercise for flattening the plane of swing, particularly for the person who slices, is to practise with the feet below the ball, perhaps a foot or so. This automatically means that the plane of swing should be more horizontal, with a shoulder turn rather than dip. Ideally this can be tried first with one of the longer clubs, perhaps a 4-iron, gradually getting the same feeling with the shorter clubs and with the ball nearer the level of the feet.

Keeping the head still

Ideally the head should stay still and the eyes look at the ball through impact. It is a common problem to find players who simply cannot keep their head still through impact. Often this is a result of holding the head too low at address. Wearers of glasses often have this problem – bifocals almost always produce quite the wrong position.

The feeling should be one of looking down the face, not with the head over in a near horizontal position. The higher the head is held at address, the easier it is to keep the head still. For the player who lifts the head, the thought must often be of standing with 'head up' rather than keeping the head down.

But what can also cause problems is the relationship of the chin and shoulders. In the backswing the left shoulder should cover the chin and almost a little of the mouth. In the throughswing the same should happen, with the right shoulder covering the chin and part of the mouth as the arms swing through and up. Players who have difficulty in keeping their head still often let the right shoulder move under the chin in the downswing, so that the chin pokes out. The right shoulder often then gives the chin a hefty punch from beneath, forcing it up. This shows up at the end of the swing with the chin out instead of tucked in. It is a fault that is particularly likely to happen for anyone with relatively narrow shoulders and a longish neck, and is therefore one from which women are more likely to suffer than men! To correct this, practise swinging back and through, with three-quarter-length swings, covering the chin on both backswing and throughswing with the appropriate shoulder. Initially opening the mouth slightly, tongue down, can make the feeling easier, pushing the chin into the right position.

Two other 'head still' exercises

For the player who drops the head into impact, the feeling needs to be of keeping the head up and stretching the arms down and out at the ball. Ideally, if a taller person can hold a clump of the player's hair from the top of the head, this does encourage keeping the head up and still – an exercise Jack Nicklaus had inflicted on him by Jack Grout. Obviously the feet need to be kept safely out of the way of the clubhead!

For the player whose head moves forward through impact the easiest way of checking this is to hold the followthrough, then to look back down to the original ball position to monitor any movement. Gradually it should be easier

Developing clubhead speed

to stay in position, combining this with active legwork.

Developing clubhead speed

To produce length to a shot the clubhead needs to move at maximum speed through impact. To produce clubhead speed there needs to be a feeling of looseness and freedom in the hands and wrists. Anyone in search of more length should loosen the grip and have plenty of practice swings, feeling the hands swishing the club through, with the right arm folding in the backswing *and* the left arm folding in the throughswing. The looser this can be, the more the weight and speed of the clubhead can be felt.

An excellent exercise for developing clubhead speed is to swing the club back and through, back and through, with a continuous action for ten or twelve swings, feeling that the arms travel a comparatively short distance but that the wrists and hands produce as full a swing back and through as possible with the clubhead. Once this feeling is achieved, strengthen the hands by this same back and through swinging in some thickish rough. Emphasis should be on the hands, wrists and forearms turning and swishing, without any feeling of power or force from the shoulders.

Finding a natural swing

The good golfer can often feel he loses his natural swing, becoming uncomfortable at address or in the swing itself. A great exercise for finding the real swing and getting rid of minor problems is to line up a row of ten or twelve balls, hitting fairly quickly one after another, setting up to each, finishing each swing, but trying to minimize thinking. By the end of the row of balls, the natural swing and address position will often return.

With the long irons the ball is ideally played fairly well forward in the stance towards the left foot. This is certainly possible where the ball sits on a good lie with grass beneath the ball. The ball can then be struck crisply with a little divot just beyond it, or swept away with a clean, nipping contact. The grip needs to stay firmly in control at the top of the backswing but, for all but strong professional players, with the wrists reasonably loose to allow the hands to release and swish the clubhead through impact (photo: Jack Nicklaus)

a

b

The contact for the fairway wood is different from that of iron shots. If the ball is sitting reasonably well the idea is to bounce the sole of the club directly behind the ball, sweeping it away from the bottom of the swing, rather than hitting it with a downward attack. As a general rule the better the lie the further forward the ball can be played and the more easily it will gather good height. From a fairly good lie the ball should be positioned a couple of inches inside the left heel, concentrating on a wide, inside takeaway, sweeping the ball away from the bottom of the swing and then extending on through to a good, full finish with perfect balance (sequence: Lanny Wadkins)

e

c

d

f

g

With the short and medium irons the aim is to hit
the ball slightly on the downswing; the shorter the
club and worse the lie the more descending the blow.
The ball is played between a third and midway back
in the stance, easing it back to encourage the more
downward attack of ball and then divot. The
backswing is controlled, working for accuracy more
than maximum speed, watching the ball well
through impact. The finish is perfectly balanced,
weight concentrated on the left heel and the tips of
the toes of the right

a

b

The direction of the swing can be seen, the body
turning to point the clubshaft parallel to the
proposed line of the shot, left arm in control. In the
perfect backswing position the clubface and left arm
follow the same angle. As the swing moves into the
hitting position the club can be seen attacking the
ball from 'inside'. At the end of the swing the body
and legs have turned to face the target, left leg
twisting to bring the hips through, clubshaft over
the left shoulder (sequence: Tony Jacklin)

e

d

f

g

3 Long Game Practice

Six Rules for Practice

Many golfers spend hours on the practice ground and achieve very little. Others spend a comparatively short period of time but produce the absolute maximum from a comparatively short session. The important point is always to make practice beneficial and constructive by sticking to a few basic rules. Here are six basic rules for helping you to extract the maximum possible benefit from your practice.

1. If you are at the stage of learning the game and are still a comparatively new golfer, make sure that you practise from good, consistent lies to encourage repetition. This will help you to groove the swing. Many long-handicapped golfers give themselves too much variation in the lie, trying to hit shots from good lies and bad lies without any rhyme or reason. As a rule it is much easier to groove a swing if you sit the ball up fairly well. Obviously there is a time and place to practise from tight lies and from bad lies but that needs a slight change in technique. One of the main problems for the club golfer is that he will tend to pick the club up too much with a steep backswing and chop down on the ball. If you sit the ball badly you are more likely to encourage this. If you sit it up reasonably well you give yourself a far better chance of encouraging the right sort of movements.

2. Always start practice sessions with one of the short to medium irons – say a 7-iron – and then work up gradually to the woods. The general rule is irons first, woods second. Club golfers often say that they have certain prob-lems with their driver or fairway woods but hit the iron shots well. What in fact happens is that errors show up far more with the longer clubs. The clubs with fairly little loft will catch the ball around its middle – the equator – and so put on lots of sidespin. The more lofted clubs naturally catch the ball below centre and produce far more backspin and less sidespin. Errors therefore show up with the long clubs which don't show up with short ones. If you start by working at sorting out problems with the medium iron, this will pay off as you work towards the long clubs. It is also as a rule far easier to get the feeling of a good swing with the irons than the woods. The irons have heavier heads and the woods the lightest, the driver being the lightest club in the set. You can usually produce better clubhead feel by starting with the irons and moving on to the woods. This also encourages good timing and is a logical progression through the set of clubs. To the professional golfer teaching you, the errors in the swing will usually be fairly apparent with a 5 or 6-iron and he will usually want to correct errors by working with these clubs first, knowing that this will then improve the longer clubs.

3. Pace yourself. Don't rush. Many golfers practise with far too many balls in their practice bag and just hit them one after another without any real object in mind. If practising on a driving range or where you have plenty of balls to hit, break the balls into fairly small groups, thinking of achieving some specific task with a group of ten or twelve balls rather than banging them away fairly mindlessly. Concentrate on quality not quantity. You will usually find pro-

fessional golfers taking time over their practice. They may start a practice session by a gentle loosening-up, hitting the balls fairly quickly one after another. But from then on each shot tends to be approached deliberately, trying to simulate as near as possible shots they want on the course. The inexperienced golfers, including many young would-be professionals, tend to think that improvement will easily happen simply by hitting a large number of golf balls. Certainly this can act as a strengthening process but may achieve very little. It is often far better to practise with one tube of twenty balls, hitting those in a meaningful way towards the target, collecting them and starting all over again. This focuses the attention on hitting each shot well rather than being careless. This is particularly important for the good golfer. The good golfer is trying to eliminate bad shots. His good shots are already there and often don't need any improvement. The single-figure-handicapped golfer's success is going to depend firstly on cutting out the bad shots and secondly on improving those bad shots that do creep in. There is no point in hitting a bad shot and then simply discounting it as though it wouldn't happen on a golf course. The good player needs to hit the balls relatively slowly, as determined as he would be on a course to get rid of unwanted shots.

4.   Always aim at a target. Sometimes you will be faced with a practice ground which doesn't have any built-in targets. Don't simply stand and hit balls down the field without any aim in mind. Always walk down the field and set up some target to aim at. In this case it is best to set the target at a specific distance, moving it or moving yourself so that the target is as nearly as possible at the correct distance. The ideal way of practising is to set out a reasonably large target which you can realistically hit from time to time. Most golfers practise to a post or to a flag but virtually every shot you hit is then going to be a failure. At best the good golfer will only hole a full shot once or twice a year. It is very easy to practise to a flag and become demoralized at shots, possibly not realizing how close they land to the target. In this way you can gradually get a sense of failure when what

you need is to boost your confidence.

An ideal target for the good player is an open umbrella, firmly stuck in the ground at the distance you aim to hit. At least you get the satisfaction of landing a ball in it from time to time and it also gives you some sort of perspective for distance so that you can gauge how many yards to the side the ball is landing. With a flag on its own, your judgement is often poor. Another way of setting up a suitable target is to put your practice-ball bag down at the correct distance, with a closed umbrella jammed in the ground say five yards to each side of this. The exact width of your target will need to vary according to the length of shots you are hitting. This would give a good target for a good player hitting medium irons and should then be expanded for the longer-handicapped player or for the good player hitting long irons or drives. In this way you can assess just how well you are doing and can begin to monitor the kind of direction you are producing. If you are setting two objects to the side of your target area I would suggest always having something else halfway between the two, such as the practice-ball bag, so that you get used to aiming at a particular spot rather than between two obstacles.

5.   If on a mission of fault finding and working through a problem, think things out logically, looking at the flight of the ball and the impact, and from there sort out any likely errors in the swing and particularly in the set-up. Make notes of your findings because almost certainly the problem will recur later. The process of sorting out problems needs to be thought out systematically. Analyse the flight of the ball in terms of where it started and how it has curved in the air. If there is a problem with the contact be specific over what is happening. In this way you can be fairly certain of what is causing this at impact and can begin to work backwards to find the error in the swing.

All too often people will make changes – both amateurs and unfortunately some professionals in their teaching – not by working through this logical process but by concentrating too much on the look of the swing. It is all too easy for people to have a set idea of what a good golf

Always practise to a target at the correct distance

swing should look like. They may have in mind Ben Hogan, Tom Watson or perhaps Jack Nicklaus. At the first sign of faults all they do is to try to spot differences between their idea of the perfect golf swing and your swing. He does this, you do that. All you do is to work at changes in the appearance of the swing which in fact have no bearing on the kind of shots you are likely to produce – and may well be counterproductive. So think logically. You should also if possible make one change at a time so that you can begin to see the benefits. If for example you think there may be an error in the ball

position, experiment with this systematically. Don't try to change the ball position and, for example, alter the grip or you won't know which, if either, is having the effect.

6. If consolidating the swing and practising for what you hope to achieve on the golf course, adopt exactly the same routine as you would on a course. Don't simply stand and hit balls, looking up once and thrashing them down the fairway, if this isn't what you do in play. If you line up shots from behind on the course then do the same on the practice ground. If you look up twice on the course do the same while

practising. In this way you are actually rehearsing what you hope to do. All too often players have one way of approaching shots on the driving range or practice ground and then do something completely different on the course. This is not just in the swing and the set-up but stems right from the way in which they walk up to each shot, grip the club, aim and so on.

Your Practice Session

There are many ways in which practice can not only be made far more interesting but can also be as productive as possible. Here are some ideas for planning each practice session for players of different standards and with different problems.

A general practice session

If you are consolidating your swing when things are going reasonably well, work up through the short irons to the fairway woods and driver. An example would be to work with a bag of sixty balls, preferably all reasonably good and worthwhile hitting. First of all work with the 8-iron, 6-iron and 4-iron. Let's assume you hit these 120 yards, 140 yards and 160 yards. The first stage is to pace out 160 yards on the practice ground and to put your practice bag or preferably an open umbrella into the ground at that point. Then go back to a distance 120 yards from the umbrella and hit a batch of twenty 8-irons. Separate the balls out into this group of twenty. Then go back another 20 yards to hit twenty balls with your 6-iron and finally back another 20 yards to hit with your 4-iron. Take the shots relatively slowly, meaning each one to go well. Line up the shots from behind or from the side in exactly the same way as you would on the golf course. If you are a club golfer you are basically looking at improving your good shots. If you are a good player your concern is far more to eliminate bad shots. On every shot try to make the swing feel balanced and hold the end of the swing until the ball is virtually landing. In a bad shot, be as specific as with a good shot in trying to hold the finish. This will

tell you if the balance is good and will give you feedback about what has gone wrong in the swing. You may, for example, see the ball pushing out to the right and find yourself with the leg action blocked and the hip simply facing out to the right. You may on a very bad shot find yourself off balance and the end of the swing should give you a good clue to what is happening.

If your twenty balls with a specific club haven't gone well or the last one or two don't produce what you want, then stick to your pattern and go on to the next shot. If in moving to the longer club you simply can't get the same feel as you did for the shorter one, then by all means go back a stage and hit a couple of shots with the shorter one to try to relate the feeling of one to the other. Having hit those balls, pick them up, moving the umbrella another 40 yards, say, for your driver, giving yourself a target 180 yards away for the fairway wood and, say, 200 yards away for your driver. Hit twenty balls of each and again make each shot count. When you collect the balls you should have a good idea of the pattern of shots you are producing and will be able to check the kind of distances the ball is travelling. The good golfer should always practise with the best possible practice balls so that he can really gauge the distance the shots are flying. If at the end of your session with the woods you have the practice ground to yourself, you can get in some short game practice by pitching the balls with your sand iron to the umbrella until they are all in a reasonably collectable group.

In this kind of session you work logically through the clubs, give yourself a target and pace things fairly slowly to rehearse what you want on the course.

Practising alignment and direction

For many golfers one of the main problems is lining up correctly. Often what happens in a practice session is that a player will hit a couple of balls down the practice ground by way of loosening up and the place where those first two balls land he will assume to be his target. Often he is simply allowing for a draw or a slice without realizing this. For all golfers, and particularly those with an alignment problem, it is essential to practise to a target. Players who have difficulty in aiming will often find that the problem is worsened in some situations. They may get an awkward feeling of having to aim across a certain fairway or from a tee which isn't pointing in the right direction. For these players it is essential to practise to a variety of targets in different directions, making a point of lining up each shot correctly and checking this if necessary with a club placed along the feet. If alignment is your problem there is often little point in putting a club down along your feet and hitting balls with this club in position. It is far better to go through your routine of lining up to a target, then putting the club down along your feet, walking down behind this and checking whether the alignment is correct. On the course you can't have any aid with a club along your feet so there is comparatively little point in doing this on a practice ground. Set four different targets to aim at across the practice ground, perhaps your practice bag, a couple of umbrellas or whatever. Take balls one or two at a time and set yourself up to the targets in turn. Alternatively you may find it just as beneficial to keep aiming at one target but to spread the balls out into four piles about five yards apart. Take two or three balls from one pile, move over to the next and so on. This may give you sufficient change in direction to simulate the problem you have on the course. One of the difficulties with aiming where you feel you are going across a set direction is that you will often fail to get the clubface and the feet travelling in the same direction. You may, for example, get the clubface on target but find it awkward to position the feet and shoulders square. If this is the case, always try to line up the shot from behind, choosing a spot in front of the ball in line with your target. Set the clubface squarely over this point and always start your lining-up process by standing feet together at right angles to the direction from ball to spot. In this way you should gradually find that you are able to cope with any awkward angles.

What is a round of golf?

Let's assume that a round of golf for a fairly good player will comprise something like fourteen drives (assuming you have four par threes), ten medium irons and say six fairway woods. In order to monitor your success rate it is worth taking the balls out in specific groups of these numbers. If practising your driving, take out fourteen balls and either hit these in two batches of seven or in one batch of fourteen, monitoring your success rate and so your progress. Similarly break the iron shots down into groups of ten, perhaps ten with a 6-iron or ten with a 4-iron and so on. Moving on to the fairway woods you can then tackle these in batches of six, monitoring a specific success rate for each group. For the good player developing a game it is an idea to keep a record of the successes of each group, knowing, for example, whether you can hit iron shots at a rate of around eight out of ten, drives at say eleven out of fourteen success rate, and so on with the fairway woods. In this way you can try to push up your success rate session after session with a specific idea of progress and with a feeling of achievement.

Varying the clubs

One of the problems for the fairly inexperienced club golfer is moving from one club to another on the golf course. Very often on a practice ground he will get into the swing of things with a certain club, finding a set pattern to the address position and gradually getting comfortable with the grip. After a few shots he probably gets himself into the right position and starts hitting the ball well. On the golf course he probably finds it very difficult to move from one club to another, part of the problem then being to get the correct set-up and to grip the club properly. For the long-handicapped player it is essential to re-grip the club properly for every shot, never simply pulling forward one ball after another with the hands remaining locked. He will also find plenty of benefit in varying the clubs, learning to take out one club and then another, quickly becoming comfort-

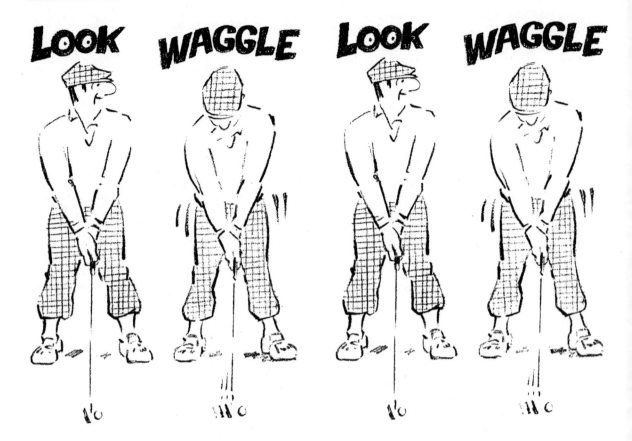

able with each. Part of his practice session should definitely be to use say five different clubs, hitting one shot with the first, one with the second and so on until he can move from club to club in a totally comfortable way.

Playing a round of golf

Another exercise on much the same lines for the club golfer is to imagine playing a specific round of golf or perhaps a few holes of that round. Again this is training him to change from one club to another and to be able to take up each club afresh without a feeling of awkwardness. This should follow a general practice routine of loosening up and hitting a few balls. He should then imagine himself playing on a specific course, starting by hitting the ball with a driver, then perhaps with a fairway wood and with a third shot with his wedge. From

there he should imagine moving on to the second hole with another driver and perhaps a 4-iron and so on. In this way he will also begin to feel any shots on that particular course which cause problems. Very often he will find that holes which cause problems in reality also cause problems on the practice ground. Again it is a good way for the club golfer to learn to feel comfortable with every club.

Adopting a definite routine

This is advice specifically for the very good golfer but has real benefits for the club player too. In order to hit the ball well it is essential to adopt as definite a routine as possible. Most golfers have far too much variation between what they do on the practice ground, what they do in play and what they do under pressure. Often their approach to shots will slow down

Developing a routine for practice and play

quite dramatically under pressure, becoming pedantic and trying too hard, often rushing the swing and bringing out the worst in their golf.

As far as possible each shot on the practice ground should be played in the same way as the shots on the course, with the same routine being used in a pressure situation. Instead of this a player will often hit balls on the practice ground in a fairly carefree way, pulling the ball towards him, looking up once and simply hitting it. On the course he probably does something quite different, lining up the shot from behind, now looking up a couple of times and fidgeting or having some other mannerism before hitting the ball. In a tournament or when tired or under pressure he probably alters this again, looking up a third or fourth time, shuffling the feet and making other unwanted movements.

The good player needs a definite routine so that he can almost set a stop watch from the moment he looks at the shot from behind to the moment he strikes it. The more repetition he can get, the better his chance of success on the course.

For the good player it is essential to practise for the real thing by hitting the balls comparatively slowly and lining up each thoroughly and systematically. Every shot should be approached as though it is the real thing. Here again the player needs relatively few golf balls, walking round behind each to line it up properly and sorting out for himself his exact routine in terms of waggling the club in preparation, looking up to the target and so on. His precise method of lining up, setting the feet and attacking the ball should be monitored fully. He should also finish the swing and watch the ball in a fairly routine way, gradually developing the repetition which is needed for good play.

Practising driving

Let's assume once again that a round of golf consists of fourteen drives (with four par threes). To practise driving really meaningfully you need to have a definite target area in mind with something to give you guidance as to whether or not your drives would land on a fairway. For the good player I would suggest having two targets 30 yards apart, and something bang in the middle to aim for. Two rolled-up umbrellas stuck in the ground can, for example, give side targets with a practice-ball bag strategically placed in the middle to aim at. The ball should then be approached in a fairly slow, routine way, working systematically at trying to get all fourteen well away and down the middle. This begins as a rule to produce a little pressure and competitive spirit even when practising on your own. You can gradually get the feel for your own success rate and monitor the accuracy of your shots.

This is then an excellent exercise for group coaching, giving players a sense of competing with each other, and the pressure of having to record their success or failure rate.

Driving a specific course

For the top-class player driving is often the most important part of the game. Without good driving he is always off to a bad start and struggling. If he is driving well, the course is made comparatively straightforward. The good player will also often want to feel that he needs to draw the ball or fade the ball or protect one side of the fairway or the other. An excellent exercise for the good player is to imagine driving a specific course, imagining himself playing the first hole, driving the second hole and so on.

Some holes will require a specific kind of feel, moving the ball slightly one way or the other. Frequently this can give the player a feeling for the real thing. Again it is much more meaningful than simply hitting one drive after the other without any set pattern or real thought in mind.

Producing a variety of shots

Many good golfers practise on the practice ground without really knowing what they are trying to achieve. Often they will practise hitting a ball perfectly straight when on the course they then prefer to hit the ball with a slight fade or perhaps a slight draw. On a practice ground they may indeed see shots with a long or medium iron as requiring a perfectly straight flight but may then get on the golf course and see everything with the ball moving slightly left to right or slightly the other way. Again they are not practising for what they want to do under pressure. In this case a good player needs to be able to feel he is building up good ball control, and should experiment with moving the ball slightly from left to right or slightly from right to left. It is a mistake to stand for too long trying to produce one particular shot in case a bad pattern to the swing is encouraged. The good player, or anyone who is trying to learn to work the ball with slight sidespin, should vary his pattern of shots to include every now and then two or three balls moved from left to right and two or three moved from right to left. A good pattern for the aspiring player is to hit two fades, two draws and ten straight shots followed by two draws, two fades and ten straight shots etc. In this way the player has to produce the correct shot the first time but without doing so many in succession that a fault is worked into the swing.

The good player's driving accuracy

As a rule the really good player is unlikely to try to hit every drive perfectly straight. He may indeed want to feel that 90 per cent of the shots are hit with a straight flight but there will certainly be odd occasions when he feels he wants to fade or draw the ball. In a situation with out-of-bounds down the left of the fairway, for example, the player who hooks the ball will often feel most uncomfortable. He feels as though he has to start the ball miles out to the right and is then almost encouraging the hook which is going to get him into trouble. In some situations he simply cannot aim way out to the

Imagine driving a specific course

right, perhaps because of a line of trees or some other problem down the right-hand side of the fairway. In this situation the player should practise with a clearly defined line or obstacle down the left of the practice ground which he imagines to be the out-of-bounds mark, and preferably with an obstacle down the right-hand side. In this way he should feel that he can aim down the left side of the fairway, moving the ball in with slight cut spin to land safely on the fairway. It is often not very constructive simply to practise this without any real target or object down the fairway. He may simply fade the ball but without any real feeling of where he is starting it, the reason for fading it and the area he is trying to land in. If he sets two targets 30 yards apart, this can encourage him to produce the correct type of shot and simulate what is going to happen on the course. He may also find great benefit from standing as

far over to the left side of the practice ground as possible and actually learning to work the ball away from the defined sides of the practice ground, perhaps a row of trees or whatever. Similarly the player who slices the ball may be very afraid of the right-hand side of the course and again is well advised to practise for this particular shot by giving himself some obstacle on the right which represents out-of-bounds or a pond, either planning on starting the ball out over it and drawing it back in or learning to hit the ball with a perfectly straight flight without allowing for and so encouraging an even worse slice.

For the good player the way of controlling the ball off the clubface with a drive is usually dependent on the relationship between the speed of the body unwinding and the clubhead. The feeling of fading the ball is usually one of unwinding the body rather early and if anything keeping the hands and clubhead slightly delayed. Conversely the feeling of drawing the ball is often one of being slightly slow with the legs and body in the unwind and speeding up the clubhead. To draw the ball the feeling is often one of having to sit slightly longer on the right foot in the change of directions at the top of the backswing, making quite sure that the clubhead reaches impact fractionally earlier in relation to the legs and body. The good player definitely needs to monitor his driving, ensuring that the ball really does start off in the direction he means and with just a touch of the correct pattern of sidespin.

Competitive practice

A good practice session should prepare the player for a round of golf and should also prepare him for a competitive situation. Those players who achieve most from their practice usually set themselves certain standards and certain tasks to achieve. Some players are able to motivate themselves very well; others, particularly youngsters, are often better in a head-to-head competitive situation. The following are therefore some ideas of competitive practices. The first two can either be done by the player on his own or competing with others and the second two competitively between players.

Driving between targets

This depends on setting two side targets, preferably about 30 yards apart, and trying to drive the ball between these two targets. The idea is simply to work at getting the most possible in succession between the two targets. The player on his own can monitor his success rate, judging his own improvement. This is also a good competitive practice particularly for youngsters. The players are all told to set up a ball and to hit the first drive. Those who succeed stay in for the second round. Those who fail stand back. The same thing happens again until there is an ultimate winner. Frequently the players who believe their driving is good and who have practised driving for an hour or so beforehand

will immediately fail once there is a competitive element. It is a good way of bringing home to the would-be tournament golfer that his or her method may not stand up to the pressure of play or competition.

Distance from a target

A good way of practising iron shots is to hit a batch of twenty balls to a target at a specific distance, giving yourself specific points for all balls within a certain distance. Give yourself, for example, four points for any ball within five yards of the target, two points for any within ten paces and one point for any within twenty paces. Again this gives you a way of monitoring your success rate, and also makes absolutely certain that each ball counts. This is often a good competition for youngsters, either where there are two or three, each having differently marked golf balls, or as a team game with two teams, again each having different-coloured balls or playing to two targets. One of the advantages with youngsters doing team practices like this is that they have to learn to play the shots with other people watching, and this adds a competitive edge.

Head-to-head driving

Another way of developing a competitive spirit with driving and for simulating pressure is to set players in a head-to-head driving competition. This can be done in one of two ways. The best way is to set two side obstacles 30 yards apart; the players take it in turns to play a drive along this imaginary fairway. They get a point for a success, with the proviso that the ball carries at least a certain distance. The second way is to have a definite target to aim for, monitoring which of them hits the ball closer in the direction of the target. With a team practice one can set up a form of knockout competition, playing off in pairs down to semi-finals and final with a head-to-head driving competition of, say, ten drives each. This again is a very good way of encouraging youngsters to think sensibly about each shot and once more puts on a bit of pressure in preparation for

Practise driving between two points, carefully monitoring your success

coping with the golf course. Some find this extremely difficult but it does bring home to them the shortcomings in their game. This can also be adapted into two teams, players taking it in turns to hit their drive in front of team members, scoring one point for a success with each player in the team hitting, perhaps, six drives. Once more there is the added pressure of having to do this in front of team members.

Competitive iron shots

Although a driving competition is usually the most popular with youngsters, an iron competition to a target can be equally beneficial if well thought out. The ideal form of practising iron shots in a competitive situation is to put an open umbrella at a specific distance, say 150 yards, with two obstacles about 10 yards to either side of this, rather depending on the standard of the players. Players are divided into two teams, let's say five per team. They take it in turns to hit one shot at a time, say six each in all, scoring five points for any ball which lands in the umbrella (not necessarily staying there) and one point for any ball which lands between the two outside marks. Again this is giving some purpose to practice and making each shot count.

For more advanced players of perhaps junior international standard an adaptation of this is to give as a target a larger area of five open umbrellas all placed together in a circle. They would then have a fairly good chance of hitting this target. The outside obstacles are again set 10 yards to the side of this. The scoring system now is to take the players in their teams, one at a time, scoring once more five points for a ball which pitches in the umbrella but losing all the points which the rest of the team has already scored for any shot which lands outside the two outside obstacles. By the last round this can put the players under heavy pressure, particularly if their team members have been building up a winning score over the opposing team.

The correct contact with the driver should be to sweep the ball away slightly on the upswing. The ball should be teed up so that the top of the driver is if anything just above the middle of the ball. The ball should then be played forward in the stance, almost opposite the left heel, with a feeling that the bottom of the swing still falls in virtually the same place but that the ball is caught several inches beyond this

a

b

If the ball sits tightly to the ground without any real cushion of grass it is necessary very definitely to bounce the sole of the clubhead on the ground just behind the ball with a slightly more U-shaped attack. If the lie is poor and any of the ball seems to nestle below ground level it is necessary to hit it with a very slightly downward attack, playing the ball back more towards the centre of the stance. In this case the clubhead can be tipped forwards slightly to bring the back of the sole of the club off the ground and to make it even easier for the clubhead to meet the ball with a true strike (sequence: Bobby Clampett)

c

c

d

f

g

a   b   c

In the address position with the driver care has to be taken to keep the weight evenly balanced between the two feet. Having the ball towards the left foot can wrongly encourage the player to set the weight towards the left foot. Instead the stance must be kept equally balanced, if anything slightly favouring the right foot, with the right shoulder quite definitely dropping below the left and the hands if anything slightly behind the ball. As the swing continues the club needs to move out on a wide path, moving back on a very definite inside curve into a full backswing position where the hands are outside and behind the head. In the backswing you should have a definite feeling of turning and staying well behind the ball, not by swaying to the right but as though by keeping the upper half of the body turned and well behind it. In the downswing the weight must be transferred very definitely backwards from the ball of the left foot to the heel of the left foot with the body turning on through to face the target; the whole centre of gravity stays well behind the ball through impact but with active leg work. The finish should be full with the shaft of the club right through onto the player's shoulder or neck, the clubhead travelling a full and complete circle with the emphasis on freedom and balance. Emphasis in driving needs to be on good timing, trying to curb any tendency to hit the ball too hard and very definitely waiting for the clubhead in its change of directions at the top of the backswing (sequence: Ken Brown)

e

f

h

i

4 Chipping and Putting Practice

Putting

There are very few hard and fast rules about putting. One point which is essential, however, is to grip the club correctly. Most putters have a flat-fronted grip which encourages the player to set the hands with the palms virtually to the side of the club and the tips of the thumbs down the front. Having set the palms in this way, most professional golfers use a reverse overlap grip with the index finger of the left hand round the outside of the fingers of the right. Any adaptations of this grip, perhaps with the index finger of the right hand down the shaft or with the hands separated, should follow this guideline, keeping the hands to the side and in particular keeping the right palm behind the putter. The putter should then be set squarely behind the ball, eyes directly over the ball, head virtually horizontal for a short putt which makes it as easy as possible to judge a straight line from the ball to the hole. In theory if the head is slightly inside this line there is a tendency to push putts and if outside the line a very definite tendency to pull putts to the left. Balance is as important in putting as in the rest of the game; the feet should be set a comfortable width apart, weight preferably evenly balanced. Ideally the putter should sit sufficiently upright and be sufficiently short to enable the player to keep the left wrist high. This encourages the wrists to stay firm throughout the stroke. A low hand position with a flat lie putter tends to produce too much wrist action.

With a short putt most good putters prefer to have the feeling of a straight back and through stroke rather than a slight curve. Others,

however, maintain that the putter must always move back on a slight curve and through on a slight curve. You cannot say that either is right but as a rule for the club golfer the straight back and through approach is easier. Good short putting depends on repetition of a sound stroke, the main rule being to keep the putter moving slowly but accelerating slightly through impact, with a very definite, stationary finish. The head should be kept absolutely still, listening for the ball to drop. The putter should move back and through comparatively low to the ground, if anything low on the backswing and with a very slightly rising stroke through impact. The putter should most definitely not brush the ground but must be kept almost as low to the ground as possible without touching it. Good short putting is a combination of reading the green well, setting the putter square to the chosen line and developing a really good stroke. On fast greens there needs to be a subtle combination of speed and direction but direction is as a rule the prime requirement.

With long putting, good results depend far more on excellent judgement of distance. As a rule a player is unlikely to be more than a few inches off the chosen line but can easily leave the ball several feet short or run it several feet past. The stroke becomes less important, many good long putters letting the hands and wrists come into play far more to produce good sensitivity and a feel for distance. Where short putting depends on repetition of a stroke, practising long putting should far more be a question of trying to get the strength right the first time and assessing line and length quickly and easily. With short putting a lot can be achieved by repeating one putt over and over again. With long putting far more is gained by tackling one putt, reading it well and judging the distance thoroughly, and then moving on to a different putt. Long putting is perhaps 99 per cent distance judgement.

General technique

Developing a routine

Short putting requires a good routine in just the same way as the long game. Here is a guide to a good routine to use. First have two practice swings, making sure that these practice swings are parallel to the line of the putt and not aimed at the hole. Next set the putter behind the ball, ensuring that it is square and sitting flat on the sole. Take up the grip afresh. At this point make sure you just lift the putter clear of the ground to ensure it is in your hands and not resting on the ground. You can set it back again to touch the ground but the putter must always be 100 per cent supported by you and not by the ground. From here you can swing it back as slowly and smoothly as you like. Move the putter straight back and straight through into a perfectly stationary finish, keeping the head absolutely still and listening for the ball to drop. On distances up to at least six feet you will be aware of the ball out of the corner of your left eye and will soon find there is no need to move the head or even move the eyes. Repeat this routine over and over again, having one or two practice swings for each putt, setting the putter head, lifting it to support it and then repeating the stroke.

Using the sweetspot

The sweetspot of the putter is the point which gives you the most solid, sound hit. If you strike the ball too near the toe of the club it will tend to twist open and if you hit it too near the heel it will tend to twist shut. First test your putter to check the sweetspot. The easiest way of doing this is to support the club between the thumb and index finger of your left hand and to tap along the face of the putter, starting at the toe

and working towards the heel, with a tee peg or small coin. At first you will feel the putter twisting and then, as you work back towards the centre of the putter face, you will find it no longer seems to twist but wants to move straight back and forward. In this area where no twisting is felt you have the sweetspot. Some putters, such as the Ping variety or centre-shafted putter, are designed to give a maximum sweetspot to keep the ball on line. Hopefully, having assessed the sweetspot, you will find that any line on the putter positioned by the manufacturer corresponds with the sweetspot. If there is no line or the two don't correspond, mark the top of the putter accordingly. You need to strike the ball reliably from the sweetspot and should practise doing so. The first way of checking this is to mark the back of a ball with lipstick or coloured chalk, striking the ball and seeing where it leaves a mark on the clubface. If too much towards the heel you may find balls missing to the left, and if too much towards the toe the chances are the odd one will be pushed.

Professional golfers will sometimes try to keep a ball to the left of the hole on a left-to-right putt by striking the ball a fraction more towards the heel and conversely with a right-to-left putt will sometimes try to keep the ball up to the right by striking it a little more from the toe.

Another sweetspot exercise

Another way of practising striking the ball from the sweetspot of the putter is to take a small square of sticky-back paper from the flap of an envelope, to stick this on the face of the putter in the right place and to hit putts on a practice green, concentrating on striking the ball from this precise spot. You can progressively work at making this sweetspot mark smaller until real accuracy with the strike is found. You can feel quite clearly the difference between striking the ball on the mark of paper or on the face of the putter, though, of course, the eyes should be firmly glued to the back of the ball and the contact fully apparent.

Practising the stroke

Ideally in the short putting stroke the putter should move back and through on a straight line or virtually straight line. One of the best ways of grooving a putting stroke is to practise perhaps with three-to-four foot putts with the shaft of another club set down outside the line of the putt so that the putter head is virtually in contact with this. If there is any tendency for the putter head to move out on the backswing it will strike the shaft of the other club and you can clearly monitor whether the putter has been kept on line both back and through. An alternative exercise is to set down two clubshafts and to practise working the putter between the two. In some ways the inside clubshaft is redundant, the main concern in the putting stroke being that the putter does not move outside on the backswing. Some professionals prefer the first routine and others the second.

Checking for squareness

Bad alignment with short putts causes more problems than almost anything else. Most people do not aim perfectly and will often find it very difficult to get the clubface naturally square to the target. Some putters are undoubt-edly easier than others. A putter with a fairly long clubhead will often be easier than a small, compact one. A putter with a flange at the back with a line or some other marking may again encourage setting the clubface square. At the first sign of any difficulty with short putting, check the squareness of the putter by holding it in what you feel to be the correct position behind the ball and then walking round behind it to check this. There is no harm in actually doing this in play, provided you are very careful not to move the putter and so knock the ball out of position. Frequently in setting the clubface from behind in a square position it will look most uncomfortably left or right from the ordinary address position. The easiest way of becoming familiar with the look of the square clubface is to practise setting up on some kind of floor surface which has clearly defined right angles marked on it. Kitchen tiles or patterned carpet can help you develop an eye for squareness, so too can lining up on a right-angled corner of a sheet of paper or card.

Checking your alignment

In order to check your natural lining-up, try this routine with a six-foot putt. Position the ball on a flat part of the green with a tee peg six

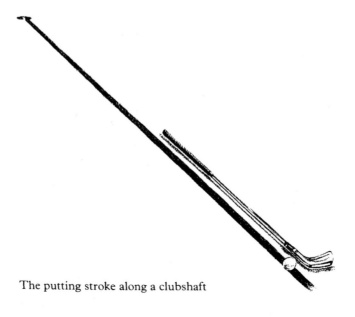

The putting stroke along a clubshaft

feet or so away. Now from behind the ball judge a line from the ball to the tee peg and position a small coin directly on this line approximately 18 inches ahead of the ball. Check from behind that all three look in a straight line. Now adopt your ordinary address position and see whether the three still look in a line. For most people who tend to aim off to the right with putts the three will no longer look in a straight line and the coin will seem displaced to the left. If for example the coin looks an inch to the left, the odds are you are wanting to aim a good inch to the right of it and so considerably right of the hole. Conversely, if the coin seems to have moved to the right, your tendency is likely to be to aim over a spot somewhat left of this. If this is the case then practise adjusting your head position, bringing the head slightly inside the line or more over the ball to see whether the three begin to look more in line. If adjusting the head makes no difference, you need to practise religiously with this three-point set-up until you can convince yourself what a straight line looks like.

Aiming over a spot

Many players who have difficulty with alignment on short putts like to adopt one of two other techniques for achieving maximum chance of squareness. The first is to choose a spot directly on line with the hole, perhaps six or seven inches ahead of the ball. For many it is far easier to set the putter square to this point rather than to the hole itself. If, having tried the three-point test above, you know that you don't naturally see a straight line, you may feel uncomfortably aimed left or right of the hole when aiming over a spot. Here again it takes repetition and possibly hours of practice convincing yourself that that spot really is on line with your chosen target, setting the putter square to it and concentrating on a stroke which sets the ball out on target. It may in turn be necessary to have someone else monitoring your putting, checking whether the ball really does start out on line. One of the difficulties with putting is that it is not always apparent why a putt misses. It may be a combination of mis-

reading a putt, mis-striking it from the wrong part of the clubface or a pull stroke which starts it off on line. Frequently you cannot tell yourself and need a second pair of eyes to give you correct feedback.

The second way of helping alignment is to position the ball so that the name on the ball is directly on line with the hole. This again can be very helpful for the person who naturally consistently aims off to one side or the other. Once more, having set the ball with its line aiming correctly you may feel most uncomfortable, but you have to trust this and concentrate on starting the ball out on this chosen line.

Keeping the head still

Good putters emphasize keeping the head as still as possible. Practise hitting a series of putts of three to six feet, ensuring that both the head and the eyes stay absolutely still until the ball drops. With putts of this distance it becomes apparent that the ball can still be seen easily from the corner of the left eye and you become aware of whether the ball drops straight in, curves in from one lip or how it misses. There is no need to look up at all but more short putts are probably spoiled by coming up on the shot than by anything else. If the head is allowed to move prematurely it is all too easy for the putter head to move off line fractionally before impact.

Firm left wrist

Most good putters advocate a firm, high left wrist through impact with short putting. As a rule the aim is to minimize the hand and wrist action to keep the putter head travelling on a straight line. An excellent exercise is to practise short putts of three to four feet with the left hand only, building up strength in the left wrist and encouraging the wrist to stay firm. As a rule a flat-fronted putter grip encourages keeping the hands to the side, left one to the front, and combined with the lie of the putter this will see the left wrist held high. There is a reason behind this, for a high left-wrist position tends to be a firm, locked one. A low left-wrist position produces too much looseness for short

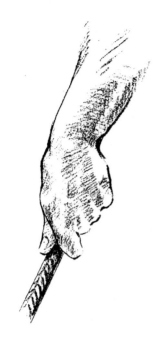

The high left wrist for putting

have far too long a backswing an excellent exercise is to practise a push stroke for putts of up to two feet six inches. In this you set the putter behind the ball and then just push the ball towards the hole with no backswing at all. This encourages the feeling of the putter head moving out towards the hole and should convince the player that the ball can move far enough with virtually no backswing. The stroke is, of course, illegal and only a practice technique. Having practised this on the putting green, you should be able to develop it into a good putting stroke by swinging the putter back a comparatively short distance, rather than having a long loose backswing.

Curing the yips

One of the main reasons for yipping with short putting is in starting off with a jerky takeaway. The general advice to the person who yips is to hold the putter lightly. Unfortunately this often allows the player to set the putter down on the ground behind the ball with the putter actually supported by the ground. In starting the backswing from this position you would have to gather the putter into the hands and swing it back all in one movement and this tends to be jerky and out of control. One of the finest exercises for curing the yips is to set the putter behind the ball and then to lift it gently into the hands, swinging the putter back from a position where it is held perhaps a quarter of an inch above the ground at address. The putter must then be firmly in the player's hands and as a rule can be swung back very smoothly. Another version of this which can help is for the player to lift the putter, to set it in front of the ball and then to return it behind the ball before making the takeaway. This exercise is often thought of as one for helping with alignment but can in fact be an ideal cure for the player who tends to start with a putter wrongly grounded instead of supported in the hands. The player who yips needs the smoothest, slowest possible putting stroke and in addition may find practising with both hands singly builds up strength in the hands and wrists which encourages smoothness.

putting, though it may in turn give feel for the long putts. Practise with five balls, setting up to each, head still and producing a smooth stroke with the back of the left hand taking the putter head firmly towards the hole. This movement can also be encouraged by putting an object such as a comb or a pencil through the watch strap on the back of the left hand, so that the left wrist receives a sharp nudge at any unwanted movement.

The push stroke

One of the faults of many poor short putters is that they swing the putter too far back and then decelerate into impact. The stroke must not be one where the backswing is too short or has a tendency to jerk and jab through impact. Ideally the stroke should be slow and controlled both back and through. For those players who

Looking at the hole

Some players become almost mesmerized by their putting stroke, failing to watch the ball properly and tending to watch the putter head instead. In practising putting you may as an exercise watch the putter stroke but should always when actually executing a shot concentrate on watching the back of the ball, the putting stroke taking second place. For the player who becomes befuddled by theory and who tends to become too concerned about the stroke, a good exercise is to practise putts between two and five feet, looking at the back of the hole rather than watching the ball at all. This soon teaches the player to become more concerned with the hole and with direction rather than analysing the stroke excessively.

Some players who tend to move their heads also advocate this as a stroke to use on the course. There have been one or two good putters who have from time to time hit their short putts while looking at the hole, feeling that it actually encourages a better, more positive stroke and gives reliable short-putting results.

Practice routines

There are several ways of practising putting, not just developing the technique but bringing in a slightly competitive edge and also simulating various situations on the course. The basic work with short putting should be done on a flat surface, to encourage a good stroke, also giving meaningful feedback as to why putts miss. The better the surface you can practise on, the more reliable the stroke you are likely to produce. On the course, however, there would have to be an element of reading the green correctly, judging distance properly and choosing an accurate spot to aim at. The various routines below give some ideas for exercises, moving on to some forms of putting competitions for practice sessions.

Reading short putts

Most players need to practise putts of three to four feet as much as possible. If you can reliably hole these you can score well. Having practised from one spot, put six balls round the hole in a circle and move right round the circle holing each in turn. On a flat green this encourages correct aiming. On a hole where there is a slight borrow it gives the advantage of some putts being slightly right to left and the others left to right. You should begin reading the putts accurately to allow correctly for the borrow.

A row of balls

Set a row of balls out from the hole, the closest approximately two feet away and each going back approximately 18 inches. Start with the closest and if you hole this, move on to the second, and again if you hole that, move on to the third and so on. As soon as you miss one, return the others to their positions and start again. By the time you get to the fifth or sixth putt there should be quite a degree of motivation to hole it. It is a good exercise, giving plenty of repetition of the short putts but a good variety of lengths. Quite often it can take several minutes before all six balls are holed and at that point you can replace the balls in their original positions, removing the closest and adding it on the end of the line to give a more difficult task.

Short-putt firmness

Ideally in a short putt the ball should enter the hole fairly firmly. This is particularly necessary if the green is less than perfect. A ball which is slowing down on its last legs tends to start wobbling off line and will take up any imperfections. If the ball misses the hole it should be moving firmly enough to travel a few inches beyond it.

For players who are tentative about short putts and tend to hit them too softly, a good exercise is to stick a tee peg or ball marker just above the can in the lip of the back of the hole, practising hitting the putt firmly enough so that it strikes the tee peg and drops in rather than just creeping in the front of the hole.

Slow or firm determines the line for short putts

Short side-hill putts

There are two ways of tackling the short side-hill putt. Let's suppose the putt has quite a break from the right. You can either aim, say, three inches to the right and allow the ball to trickle gently into the right-hand part of the hole or you can hit the ball firmly straight at the middle of the hole and iron out the borrow. Many good short putters, like Tom Watson, attack the ball firmly and ram the ball at the back of the hole. Others will take a more tentative approach. Any player lacking confidence with short putting is unlikely to want to attack the putt firmly.

One danger is that players practise on the putting green a firm, aggressive approach and then do something completely different on the course, where they become nervous and defensive. There is a time and place for both approaches. In a match-play competition where you have a putt for a half you may as well strike the ball firmly and go for the back of the hole. With a putt for a win you may prefer to be conservative, and in a stroke-play competition you will want the slower putt with more borrow. On the putting green there should be two distinct ways of approaching the short putts. Give yourself a definite routine of practising some short side-hill putts, first playing a batch of short putts firmly for the back of the hole and then playing another batch with a conservative approach where you concentrate on a combination of line and length.

Aiming for a small target

Some players will come in from a round of golf, having putted well, saying that the hole looked the size of a bucket. A good way of giving yourself confidence with putting is to practise to a far smaller target so that the hole then looks comparatively large. There are several ways of doing this. A good practice routine for indoors is to practise putting to a matchbox, firstly broad side on and then narrow side on for pinpointing accuracy. Start first with short putts and then work up to medium-length putts of eight to ten feet. Similarly on the putting green put a tee peg in the ground and practise to that. This can then make the hole seem comparatively large and a putt much more inviting. Another way of tackling this, becoming progressively more difficult, is to start with two tee pegs four inches apart, concentrating on getting the ball between these and then moving it down until the pegs are just two inches apart, barely giving enough room for the ball to move between them. This can in fact be done with tee pegs just in front of the hole, blocking off part of the hole to give a really small entrance. This exercise can again be started with short putts of three feet, gradually working up to medium-length ones of eight feet.

Putting to a small target

Long-putt practice

Long putting is a question of producing perfect feel for distance combined with reading greens accurately. As a rule most players on a practice green do not spend much time in actually reading putts but tend to hit one putt and then simply learn from this in making an adjustment to direction for the next one. They ought to be reading each long putt really accurately and trying to get both distance and direction right the first time. Long putting isn't like short putting where repetition of the stroke is one of the keys to success. It is judgement and feel with long putts. An ideal long-putt practice session is to have the green to yourself and to keep putting to different targets, with different lengths and varying borrows. Each putt needs careful consideration, looking from behind to judge the borrow and then considering the putt from the side to see whether it is uphill or downhill. Often from behind the ball you can be deceived. The correct routine should then be to have a couple of practice swings, making sure that the putter doesn't brush the ground, possibly looking at the hole rather than down at the ground as you have these practice swings to feel the sort of distance you are trying to produce. Choose the correct line and make sure you really pinpoint the spot you are aiming at. Then while aiming in the right direction concentrate almost 100 per cent on running the ball the right length rather than being obsessed with the direction. You are likely to be very little out with this but can be many feet out with the judgement of length. If a putt finishes a few inches to the left or right but is the right length it is a good putt. If the line is perfect but the length wrong it is a bad one. Don't then seek to repeat the putt to get it right a second time. That is meaningless. Move on to a new situation and concentrate on judging that one.

Practising different lengths

Spend as much time as possible on a putting green practising long putts of varying lengths. Simply choose a spot on the green, not necessarily a hole, and putt a ball to it. Then choose another spot and putt to that and then to a third. Just keep working your way all over the green and around the green, working at distance judgement until you can really get it right. If you putt towards a hole and are either short or past the hole, make an assessment in inches of how far short or past you are. Then check whether your judgement of this is right when you go to retrieve the ball. Gradually you will learn to see what distance around the hole looks like. Very often the view is so foreshortened that your judgement is relatively inaccurate. You may think the ball has run perhaps two feet past and find it four feet past. You may think you have left yourself perhaps nine inches short and find it is two-and-a-half feet short. Get used to making a good assessment of the distance round the hole to build up your accuracy and judgement.

Checking your long-putt striking

Very often players will get inconsistent distance with their long putts because they don't strike the ball at the same level. Ideally the putter should strike the back of the ball firmly with the same part of the putter head. The putter should never brush the ground as it travels through but should go through almost as close to the ground as possible. Players who get inconsistent length will often catch the odd putt too

near the top of the ball and may very occasionally just make contact with the ground. In this way the ball doesn't run a consistent length and the strike needs checking. If you strike the ball accurately with a repetitive action you should be able to look at a target, hit the first ball and then without looking up again hit the second and the third to approximately the same length. In a similar way you should be able to close your eyes and strike three balls, one after another, to the same sort of distance. If your length with long putts is poor, check first of all whether the striking is accurate. You may in addition not be striking the ball from the middle of the clubface each time and may need to refer to one of the exercises in short-putting techniques to monitor this. It is well worth also having someone watching your putting stroke from virtually ground level to assess the accuracy of your strike. If you do have any problems on this line it is essential to use a fairly deep-faced putter where the contact is likely to be consistent. A shallow-faced putter can give too much inaccuracy and variation.

Putting to a string

Long putting centres around good judgement of distance. Most players become too obsessed with direction and pay insufficient detail to the distance. A good way of practising long putting

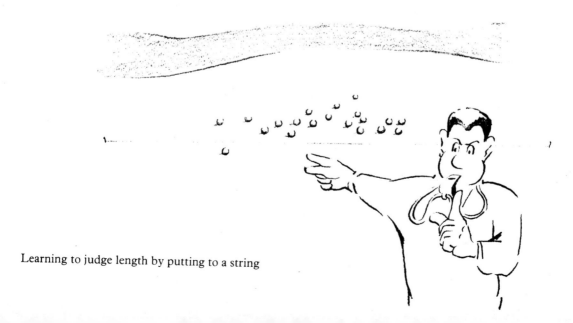

Learning to judge length by putting to a string

is to take a piece of thin string, make two loops and put a tee peg in either end, pegging this into the ground. Then practise putting from various distances, trying to run the ball as close as possible to the string, preferably trying to get it just to run over the string. In this way you begin to see distance as all-important. You may like to imagine this piece of string, say, nine inches beyond the hole and imagine the ball as close as possible to that length. If you can accurately run the ball to this distance it should give you a sound feeling of a long putt which always reaches the hole, with a chance of dropping, but then stops within a very safe return-putt distance.

To give yourself a different form of target you can set the string out in an approximate circle on the green, practising putting the balls into this from various distances. Again this should give you a picture to work with on the course, trying to get the ball to finish in an imaginary circle and therefore within this close range of the hole.

Competitive practices

Playing round the putting green

A simple way of practising your putting is to play the nine holes or eighteen holes on your putting green. Keep a card and don't give yourself anything. Finish off even the shortest of putts. This should give you the feeling of wanting to get the long putts in and yet some good practice with the short ones if your long putts aren't up to standard. Make sure that you read each putt properly. As well as doing this on your own you can of course play either a medal competition or a head-to-head match-play competition against an opponent for added pressure.

Laybacks

Another way of playing round a putting green, either on your own or against an opponent, is to play 'laybacks' and to add a little spice to your short putting. In this situation every time you miss the hole you move the ball back another putter length in the direction of your putt. In other words if you miss the hole by one foot you are going to move it back in that same direction to make it four feet away. You literally continue with this on each hole until the ball is holed out. This means that at some stage you are going to hole a putt of at least three feet or more. You can play this quite simply with a straightforward stroke-play round for your own enjoyment or as a stroke-play competition against an opponent. For good players it can also be another way of playing a few holes on the golf course for a little more competitive edge.

Consecutive successes

Another way of practising putting, particularly of a medium length, is to set a putt of a specific distance, say twice the length of your putter, and to putt ball after ball from this spot, counting the number of consecutive putts you can make before missing one. At this point start again, trying to better your score each time. This can be played in a competitive way at the end of your practice session between players, working at a set putt in a five-foot to eight-foot range. This again can emphasize to players whether or not they are able to stand up to even a small amount of pressure. Frequently, while being watched by others or with a competitive edge, those who perform well in ordinary practice will find the task more difficult.

Long-putt practice

Long putting requires good judgement the first time. One of the best ways of practising putting is on an ordinary green with just one hole, putting from various points on the green, reading each carefully and really making it matter. Spread six balls round a green for fairly long putts and aim first at getting each within the length of your putter from the hole (between 32 inches and three feet). Once you feel you can do this fairly consistently, aim for getting each within the length of the leather – i.e. from the clubhead to the bottom of the grip. There should be a sense of achievement if you can get all six long putts even within the length of the putter shaft and certainly within the length of the leather.

As a competitive exercise this can be adapted for teams of players, again putting pressure on good players to prepare them for a tournament situation. In this case divide the players into two teams, let's say five to a team. Set five putts of varying lengths around the edge of the green. The players are then numbered 1 to 5. Player 1 from each team tackles the first putt, player 2 from each team the second and so on. The player scores four points for his team if he gets the ball in the hole, two if within the length of the leather and one if within the length of the putter. Start this first with three rounds so that for the second and third putts five different putts are chosen or alternatively players move round to attempt a different one from their previous putt. The team with the most points obviously wins. Having tried this with two teams for perhaps three rounds it is then worth adapting this so that for two or three further rounds the scoring system is the same except that if any putt is outside the length of the putter from the hole the team immediately loses all its points scored by previous players! This really will have players concentrating, again simulating tournament pressure.

A pairs match

A simple pairs match with a difference is for players to alternate choosing spots around the green for fairly long putts, the player coming closer winning one point. This can be made, for example, the best of twenty-one putts.

The length of string

A good competitive practice for the end of a training session is to put down a six-foot length of string on the green, pegged into the green with two tees. Players then tackle a long putt with the idea of getting the ball as close as possible to the distance of the piece of string with the proviso that it must pass the string and

finish short of some other obstacle, say the flag stick, a further six to eight feet away. Players all put a small amount of money in a kitty, the one who finishes closest to the string taking the kitty; anyone short of the string pays double and anyone hitting the flag stick pays double. Alternatively for younger competitors a small prize can be offered for the one closest to the string, with some sort of penalty – say running the length of the practice ground – for any player short of the string or hitting the flag stick.

A team game with long putting

Two pieces of string set out on a green, say four feet apart, can give another way of playing a competitive practice. The players are divided into two teams and have to strike a long putt which finishes between the two lengths of string to score a point for their team. This can be made progressively more difficult by setting the lines of string closer together. This can also be adapted by not just scoring points for a success but losing all the team points for a failure. Once again the competitive side of practice will bring out the best in some players and the worst in others. This way of judging distance to a piece of string is an ideal practice indoors, competitively or on your own. Two pieces of thread about a yard long and, say, 18 inches apart can act as quite a reasonable target for distance, again varying the distance apart according to the player's standard.

Crazy golf

A good competition, particularly popular with juniors, is to set out a crazy-golf course on the putting green. This requires quite a bit of work from a friendly greenkeeper with a white line marker, but holes can be set out to play as severe doglegs, marking out the perimeter of each hole so that the player has to keep the ball within each out-of-bounds boundary. Any ball going over a white line has to be replayed. This is an excellent way for teaching players really good distance control, for the ball has to be judged carefully into specific spots, combined with

Crazy golf with a white line marker

holing some very testing short putts. The illustration shows a few examples of holes used. They can provide an excellent means of practice and as well as being fun can build up considerable control and feel.

Chipping

Little shots from the edge of the green can be divided into two specific shots, chipping and pitching. Pitching is dealt with in the next section. Chipping is basically a little running shot played with one of the medium irons, where the idea is to loft the ball just a few feet so that it touches down and runs the rest of the way. The ideal club for most players to use is either a 6 or a 7-iron and the feeling of the technique should be as near as possible to that of putting. The main difficulty for the club golfer is in playing the shot with firm enough wrists. The very good golfer will often play this shot almost entirely with the hands and wrists

if the lie is good enough, but as a general rule it is far better to learn a shot which is similar to putting, the left wrist in particular staying firm through impact. Any player who has a strong grip, with the left hand on the top of the club and the right at all beneath, will usually need to adapt this grip quite definitely for chipping, setting the hands far more to the side of the club than for his usual game, with the thumbs a little more down the front and so closer to the grip used with a putter. Good players are able to chip by standing comparatively close to the ball, keeping the hands and wrists up and forward. The higher the left wrist is kept at address, the firmer the wrist action is likely to be. For the long-handicapped player it is often advisable to feel that the club is balancing well up towards its toe so that the left wrist can be kept fairly high. The ball is then positioned towards the toe of the club to give good feel and the stroke is more or less like a putting stroke, keeping the elbows fairly well tucked into the body but just swinging the club back and through on a small, saucer-shaped arc. The weight should favour the left foot throughout but the ball should be struck fairly cleanly and not with a pronounced downward blow.

One of the most common mistakes of club golfers is to hold the club in the normal way and simply slide the hands down the club towards the bottom of the grip without changing the lie of the club. The hands will often then be low with the wrists dropped and this produces an unsuitably wristy action. Most good golfers will execute this shot with both feet turned slightly towards the target, left foot withdrawn slightly to produce an open stance, knees out slightly towards the target but with the shoulders fairly square. This gives a good feel for getting the ball towards the hole in much the same way as one would turn to face the hole if rolling a ball towards it.

In a good chipping stroke the backswing and the throughswing should be of virtually identical length. The judgement of distance in chipping with a 6 or 7-iron is usually very much like that of putting. If you have a couple of practice swings, imagining you have a putter in your hand, you should find that you swing the club back just about the right length. In many situations there is no need to loft the ball right onto the edge of the green. All you need to do is to set it off over any little inaccuracies that are in front of you, but the ball can then still touch down on the apron of the green if smooth enough or on the green itself if the fringe is at all shaggy. The hands should always be kept a little forward in chipping so that the club face is hooded a little – the 7-iron sitting with a loft of perhaps a 5-iron. Learning to use one club really well gives a good general-purpose shot. You only really need to alter this when you need a little more carry in relation to a little less run. At this point you may need to work up to the 8-iron or 9-iron to change the ratio of carry to run, eventually moving up to the pitching wedge or even the sand wedge and on to short pitching.

General technique

The long-handicapped player first needs to con-

centrate on keeping the left wrist firm through impact. The fault of the long-handicapped player is usually one of stopping the left wrist just before impact and letting the right hand take over. This is often in an attempt to scoop the ball into the air. For the long-handicapped player the easiest way of developing chipping is to make it as close as possible to putting. It is often better for him to use a square stance, and possibly even adopt the same grip as for a putter, perhaps with a reverse overlap grip or with the right index finger down the back of the club. The club should be balanced up towards its toe, giving the same sort of lie as a putter. The player will then often find that he can simply play a few shots with a putter and then a few with a 6 or 7-iron and transfer the feeling from one to the other.

By having the club sitting up in this way the player learns to keep a firm left wrist and begins to experience how easily the ball will rise simply

Chipping – pencil in the watchstrap for firmness

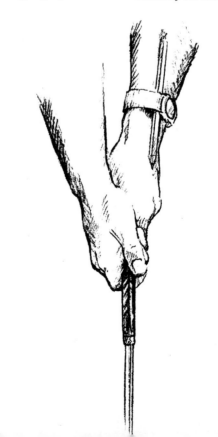

Chipping from the toe to encourage feel

by brushing the ground on which it sits. He can then work at firming up the left wrist even further if necessary by putting a comb or pencil down the back of the left wrist through the watch strap, to alert him if the wrist is allowed to collapse.

Mirroring backswing and throughswing

One of the dangers for the long-handicapped golfer is of swinging too far back with chipping and then slowing down into impact. Ideally backswing and throughswing should be the same length. One of the best ways of learning this is to set some obstacle which limits the length of the backswing and then check the length of the throughswing. You can for example position a practice-ball bag a couple of feet behind the ball, feeling that the backswing must then be short enough to enable you to accelerate gently through the ball. The stroke must not be jerky but backswing and through-swing should be virtually the same length. Stop in a stationary position at the end of the swing to check it by comparison with the backswing. This may need someone else monitoring you. One of the best ways is for another player to hold two clubs out, limiting the length of the backswing with one and setting where the limit of the throughswing should finish with the other.

Using the toe of the club

A golf club is designed to produce power. In the long game you want to hit the ball from the middle of the clubface. In chipping you want to encourage good feel. Frequently you will find that you can produce a much softer feel with chipping if the ball is kept well up towards the toe. This is particularly necessary for players who stand fairly close to the ball and if anything balance the club towards its toe end. Most good golfers usually do this to some extent, often without knowing it. The toe of the club will give a soft feel and often give a much better chance of consistent chipping. Another point to bear in mind is that the ball will often look closer to the toe of the club than it really is. Frequently you find players addressing the ball at what looks like the middle of the clubface to them. When they walk round behind to check it, it is obvious that the ball is too near the heel of the club. Players who get inconsistent distance with chipping often have the ball far too near the heel and the ball springs off from time to time with much too much speed. It may not actually come off the socket but the control is lost.

An excellent way of checking the strike with chipping is to set out a row of ten balls, less than an inch apart. Start at one end and work systematically along the row, striking each ball cleanly without touching the next one. Any player who is at all prone to hitting the ball too near the heel of the club will find this almost impossible and will from time to time hit both balls. It will also usually drive home to players just how good and soft the feel from the toe of the club can be. For any player who does from time to time shank the ball with a chip or more likely with a short pitch, this exercise can be adapted to give a better clubface/ball relationship and contact.

Learning the little ones

The difficulty most club golfers have with chipping is in being able to control really short chips. Often they simply are not delicate enough with a 6 or 7-iron and find a short shot particularly awkward. Obviously in many situations you would simply putt from just off the edge of the green, but sometimes the grass is a little too long or the surface too wet and a chip is necessary. One of the best ways of learning to chip well is to practise at home on a carpet. The shot should be built up from a tiny one of six to eight feet or so, gradually giving

the feeling that you can control a 6 or 7-iron for tiny distances in just the same way as with a putter. Many of the same exercises can then be used, chipping to a matchbox, judging chipping to a length of thread and generally practising good ball control. Tiny shots are the basis of the short game; it is far easier as a rule to build up from a little shot than work down from a longer one. By practising indoors the player is also encouraged to get a really good contact, just brushing as lightly as possible the little piece of carpet on which the ball sits, or taking the ball completely cleanly, without any downward attack. For a long-handicapped player who has difficulty in convincing himself that the ball will rise without his help, a simple way of learning the chipping contact is to approach these shots as though playing a putt, trying to push the ball along the ground with no feeling of trying to make the ball rise. Soon the player becomes aware that the ball automatically lifts and can derive no end of help from short sessions with a 7-iron and putter, making the two feel virtually identical and feeling the ball react to both clubs.

Practising tiny chips and pitches for added control

A good player's exercise

The good golfer should aim at holing most little chips from off the edge of the green. As a rule I would suggest having the flag out and thinking as positively about short chips as long putts. A good way of building up a feeling for holing the ball with a 7-iron is to practise on the practice putting green itself. This is not an exercise for the club golfer who could damage the green. The good player will find it very beneficial. Line up a row of balls on the green itself, the closest about six feet away and the rest going back two feet at a time. Start with the closest and aim to chip this in. Then work back along the row of balls, gradually feeling how easy it is to get the ball in the hole in just the same way as with a putter.

What this also encourages is a clean, repetitive contact, emphasizing that the putting contact is not a downward one with a tiny divot but a far cleaner, more sensitive one, sending the ball running as accurately as from the face of a putter. This exercise can be done in a similar way by the handicapped golfer on the carpet at home, aiming to a matchbox or some other slightly larger target. Again it builds up a feeling for being able to get the ball in the hole and a good, reliable contact.

Practice routines

Varying the distance in chipping as in long putting is very much a question of developing feel in the hands combined with hours of practice. One element is to get a really good and consistent strike on the ball and the second is then to judge distance in the same way as you would with a putter. It must be done right first time.

One of the best ways of practising chipping is to set yourself up on the edge of the green with four different targets in mind, playing to one target, then to the second, then the third and the fourth. Try to judge these shots correctly and then move on to another spot. Again just keep working at distance till you feel you can get it right first time.

Working to a target

Practise chips of different lengths rather than simply going to the hole on the green you are using. I would suggest learning chipping with a distance of about seven or eight yards. This requires a fairly delicate strike without being too short. If the hole isn't at this length, put down a tee peg or other small object and practise chipping to this. Use five balls and first aim to get all five within the club length. Once you can achieve this, aim at getting all five within the length from the clubhead to the bottom of the grip. Work systematically from one point and when you feel you have mastered that, go on to another. This exercise should give the medium- and high-handicapped player a real feeling of being able to control the ball, working at the stroke to get a consistent strike and roll to the shots.

Chipping in

It is important to have a positive feeling about getting the ball in the hole. This is particularly essential for the good player, who should practise chipping with the flag out of the hole for anything up to perhaps 15 yards. Put the flag stick down say five feet behind the hole. Take six good balls and try to get each one in the hole, feeling that each must reach the hole but stop before striking the flag stick. This should begin to produce a really positive feeling, preferably working first with fairly short chips of about five yards and building up to a distance of 15 yards.

Chipping and putting

A good routine is to combine chipping and putting. Position six balls around the green and try to get each down in a chip and one putt. You can either do this with all six balls from the same place or preferably with the chips from a different position. The first is probably more beneficial to the club player and the second to the good golfer. Now there is not only emphasis on getting the ball close but on holing a short putt as well. The good golfer in a similar way can work at the number of consecutive chips and one putts he can produce, once more either doing this from the same position or varying the shots played. This can be adapted as a head-to-head competition, the first one failing to get down in a chip and putt losing. The way of scoring this obviously needs to vary according to the standard of player and the likelihood of failing to get down in a chip and a putt.

Competitive practices

A pairs challenge

A head-to-head chipping competition is often a good way of finishing a training session. Players choose in turn the position to chip from, the one finishing closer to the hole from each position winning one point. This can be developed with good facilities to extend to chipping, short pitching and bunker shots around a certain green. Players go through, say, twenty-one rounds, tossing for who chooses first and from there choosing the positions alternatively. This can be done as a simple head-to-head competition or in a form of knockout for four or eight players.

Chipping to a jack

A good chipping competition is to play a game similar to bowls. Each player has four balls, preferably one using white and the other using yellow, but there can be more than two players. The first one hits a ball of a third colour, say red, which becomes the target. Players then chip to this ball, the idea being to finish as close as possible to it, if necessary knocking the opponents' ball away or knocking the jack (the red ball) into a better position. Players take it in turns to play a ball at the jack, and the one finishing closest after all balls have been played scores one point. If he has two balls closer than any of his opponents he counts two points, if three closer than his opponents he counts three

points, and so on. The first one to reach fifteen points wins. To make this as definite as possible the striking area for playing each shot should give the player approximately two feet leeway so that he can take a slightly different angle towards the jack.

Chipping to a string

Another competitive practice popular with juniors is to chip to a length of string. The one who finishes closest to the string wins unless his ball is short of the string. Anyone finishing short receives some sort of penalty, running the length of the practice ground or some slightly unpleasant task. You can soon distinguish those who would at all costs avoid the forfeit, making sure they don't finish short, from those who will go for success and take risks. Again this teaches good distance judgement and really fine control, combined with training a competitive spirit.

A chipping team game

Players are divided into two or three teams of even numbers. Each team is given a chip to play of approximately the same length to a hole, the flag being taken out. One point is scored every time a player gets a ball in the hole. Players have, say, four chips each depending on time and the number per team. This can then be adapted with a different scoring system as follows. A player receives four points for getting a ball in the hole, two for being within the length of the leather (clubhead to grip) and one point for being within a club length. Having had a couple of rounds of this, which usually proves very enjoyable, the competition can then be changed slightly for good players, with the same points for getting the ball in the hole or being within the length of the leather but losing all the team's points if a chip fails to get within a club length! Again this puts on pressure and brings out the best in those who are naturally competitive – to others it brings out the worst!

Putting from behind. Ideally the line of the eyes should be directly over the ball to make it as easy as possible to line up. If the eyes are inside the ball the tendency may be to push putts; if outside, a serious danger of pulling putts. The hands are kept fairly high with the left wrist arched to encourage a firm left wrist throughout the stroke. Although standing comparatively tall, you hold your head in a horizontal position, allowing it to swivel back and through to gauge the line of the putt rather than turning and lifting. In a short putting stroke the feeling is one of moving the putter back and through on a straight line, with a definite finish to the stroke, head held absolutely motionless (photo: Nick Faldo)

Putting from the front. There are very few hard and
fast rules about putting. These illustrations show
a standard grip for putting, thumbs down the front
of the club, palms of the hands to the side. The
wrists are held comparatively high with the left wrist
slightly arched, head directly over the ball and the
weight evenly spread. On a short putt the putter
head moves more or less straight back and through,
the head staying still, listening for the ball to drop
into the hole

Chipping from the front. Chipping should be thought of as being as near as possible to putting. The hands should again be predominantly to the sides of the club, as for a putter, with the wrists held slightly up and forward. This again encourages firm wrist action. The weight favours the left foot, the club being swung back and through the same length each way. There is no breaking of the wrists on either backswing or throughswing

Chipping from behind. To chip well the ball should be played fairly close to the feet, the club held up slightly to achieve this. This means that the clubhead will be balanced slightly more towards the toe of the club with the ball also positioned slightly more towards the toe. With the wrists held up in this way the wrist action is firm and crisp. The shot can either be played with a square stance, feet parallel to the shot, or with both feet and knees turned slightly towards the target, left foot withdrawn a little. The shoulders should be kept square. The feeling of the shot is of swinging the club virtually straight back and through but it does in reality move back and through on a slightly inside curve

5 Pitching and Bunker Play

Pitching: General Technique

Pitching must be divided into two definite shots, approach pitching and short pitching. The approach pitch of say 30 yards to 100 yards is played with a 9-iron, pitching wedge or sand wedge – the sand wedge from below 55 yards or so. The shot must be played with a downward, accelerating attack, keeping the ball just behind the centre of the stance, setting the hands ahead of the ball at address and with the hands and wrists slightly down. This gives an in-built wrist cock. With the ball back in the feet most players find it necessary to turn both feet to the left, possibly withdrawing the left foot slightly into an open stance but with the shoulders square. The left hand and wrist are kept firmly in control, adding slightly to the wrist cock on the backswing. In the throughswing weight must be very definitely pushed onto the left foot so that the ball is hit with a downward attack and never with the idea of helping it upwards. The left wrist is kept firm so that at the end of the swing the right hand never flicks the club through or overtakes the left. At the moment of impact the left wrist is leading with the right wrist still cocked back on itself. Although the finish is short and punchy there must still be sufficient acceleration through the ball for a good ball/divot contact. The left arm, although straight beyond impact, stays reasonably tight into the body without stretching away out to the target. The shot often becomes progressively more difficult as it becomes shorter, many players finding it helpful to move to a sand wedge for the 30- to 50-yard range.

For a short pitch up and over an obstacle the long-pitch method can be adapted still further using the sand wedge, breaking the wrists and punching the ball through. Although this method is used a lot by professionals it is generally very difficult for the club golfer, who will often decelerate and fluff the shot. The easiest way to approach a short pitch, providing the ball sits above the ground and not in a depression, is to hang both arms straight, elbows tucked into the side and with the full loft on the clubface. With the upper arms and elbows firmly locked into the body, the clubhead can be swung back and through in a short, shallow arc, simply brushing the ground on which the ball sits, with no wrist action at all. In a throughswing the arms are kept into the side, the legs active through the ball, producing a short finish where the wrists remain firm and the clubface looks upwards. It is almost as though the clubhead slides between the ball and the ground; the judgement of depth is all-important. Before playing this shot, particularly from a tight line, you should have a couple of practice swings to ensure that the sole of the club is going to brush the ground at the right level.

Pitching Exercises

The firm left wrist

Both good short pitching and good long pitching depend on the club golfer keeping the wrists firm and in particular having a firm left wrist which is not overtaken by the right hand before or through impact. A lot of benefit can be derived from practising the pitching action with the left arm alone, working to a firm-wristed position beyond the ball in both but with the upper arms still staying fairly tight to the body. Ideally the lower-handicapped player should be able to do both shots with the left hand alone with the ball.

Watching the ball

One of the difficulties for most players is that the shorter the shot, the more likely they are to look away from the ball just before impact. The ball is going to be in the air a relatively short time and this often pulls the player up far too soon. With long pitching, a good exercise for the medium- and high-handicapped player is to hit shots and then resist completely the temptation to look up. Many players find this virtually impossible to start with. This should be developed until the player can safely hit the shot, wait a good two to three seconds beyond

impact and then lift his eyes. With a long approach pitch there is always the slight fear that you may not see where the ball goes. With short pitching of 20 yards and below, an excellent practice exercise for every standard of player is to hit the ball and then keep the head still until the ball is heard to land on the green. This is the way a short pitch should really be played on a golf course; if you can exaggerate it slightly in practice the odds are that on the course the eyes are still kept focused on the ball through impact and on the ground beneath it once the ball has gone.

The short-pitch action

The short pitch of up to 20 yards over a bunker causes club players more problems than almost anything else. As a rule they tend to swing the club too far back and to slow down into impact. Provided the whole ball sits above the ground, the easiest way of playing the shot is with an action which requires no wrist action at all. Clamp your elbows into the side, the clubshaft sitting straight up towards you with the full loft

Arms tied to the body for firmness in short pitching

of the club. The clubhead is then swung back and through, brushing the ground on which the ball sits. The shot should be played with a sand wedge rather than a pitching wedge, for the sole of the sand iron is meant to produce a bouncing contact where a pitching wedge can cut into the ground unsatisfactorily. This shot should not be entirely from the shoulders but requires fairly active leg work despite the short length of the shot. Many players, in trying to produce a stiff-wristed action, will leave the legs and feet still and swing the arms away from the shoulders so that the club incorrectly leaves the body. An excellent way of learning the shot is to get someone to tie a piece of string around your body and arms at the elbows, which forces the elbows into the sides. Swinging the clubhead back and through, the top of the clubshaft then stays fairly close to your stomach, while the legs have to move through to work the arms and clubhead. With the arms tied to the body they cannot work away from the side. The player will soon find the action fairly simple and can then produce the shot unaided, still keeping the elbows in.

The short-pitch landing spot

To play a good short pitch you need to choose the spot on which the ball lands. Players will often have two problems, in choosing the correct spot and in landing on it. Part of short-pitching practice should be to choose that landing spot accurately. First look from behind the bunker you are going over, choose the landing spot and tell yourself what distance away it is from the hole; then walk up to see whether your judgement is correct. Players will often find that they choose a landing spot which is well short of the flag, but with practice they are more easily able to assess the distance round the hole and judge the spot. From there it is a question of hours of practice trying to get the ball to land on the chosen spot.

Opening the clubface

Producing good height with small pitches and then with bunker shots with the sand wedge requires the clubface to be open. This often causes severe problems for the club golfer. One of the best ways of learning to play bunker shots is to be able to play a small cut-up shot from grass, keeping the clubface open. Practise this by setting the face of the sand wedge square, with the shaft of the club directly up towards you so that it has its natural loft. Then, without gripping the club, simply rotate the shaft so that the loft of the club increases and the clubface turns away to the right through an angle of perhaps 15 to 20 degrees. At this point grip the club with your normal grip, ensuring that the right hand is kept well behind the shaft of the club rather than beneath it. Turn your whole set-up and the clubface round to the left until the bottom groove on that clubface aims at an imaginary target. Care has to be taken that the ball still appears towards the middle to toe of the clubface. The clubface may look to be in an awkward position and the grip may feel slightly uncomfortable in your hands. With the clubface almost lying on its back, and with your knees relaxed and far more bent than during other shots, have the feeling of sliding the clubhead back and through, as though sliding it beneath the ball. Practise this from a grassy lie with at least a half-inch cushion of grass beneath the ball. Practise getting the feeling of the clubhead sliding between the two until the ball seems to pop up with backspin. By having the knees well bent you should be able to keep the clubhead low to the ground both back and through to produce this sliding contact. The wrists should be firm through impact, the left wrist and left elbow definitely leading. In this way you should begin to feel the cut-up spin which is necessary for bunker shots.

Practice Routines

Short pitching

The essence of good short pitching is to land the ball on your chosen landing spot. One of the difficulties is that with a short shot there is a tendency to look up too soon, knowing that

Listening for the ball to land with short pitching and bunker shots

the ball is only in the air perhaps a second or so. A good way of practising short pitching is to practise to a target where you can definitely hear whether the ball lands correctly. In this way you should be able to resist looking up too early to see the results. The shot to practise is anything from seven yards to about 20 yards; the shorter the shot the more difficult it will often be. An ideal target is an open umbrella stuck in the ground, an old car tyre or a tin tray, all of which make a noise if you are successful. This is a shot which can be practised in the garden; again you can derive a great deal from learning the short shot and then working up to the slightly longer one.

Short-pitch practices

Having learned the basic short-pitching action it is necessary to be able to assess distance really well, judging it correctly the first time. An ideal set of targets for pitching and, as we will see, for bunker shots is a set of children's hoops about 24 inches in diameter. To practise short pitching set out four, five or six hoops at varying distances from six to 25 yards and practise going from one to the other in turn. In doing this, try to develop a definite routine, having either one or two practice swings before each, feeling the clubhead brushing the ground, looking up a specific number of times before each shot and working at getting a good finish with the eyes focused on the ball right through impact and on the spot beneath after it is gone.

Long pitching

Long pitching again requires good distance judgement. One of the difficulties with long pitching is that distance on a practice ground can be very deceptive and can look quite different from distance on a golf course. A 50-yard pitch may look a completely different task on the practice ground than on the golf course with the green and bunkers between you and the flag. In practising long pitching, assess the distance you are playing to, either measuring off the distance in paces or at least assessing it along the ground in 10-yard hops. An excellent way of practising pitching and knowing the feeling of different distances is to lay clubs in front of you at 30 yards, 40 yards, 50 yards and so on up to 100 yards, trying to land on them in turn and getting the feel of a shot of a specific distance. Most professional golfers pace off distances on the golf course and for pitches of between 50 and 100 yards will still often want to know the precise distance so that they gauge

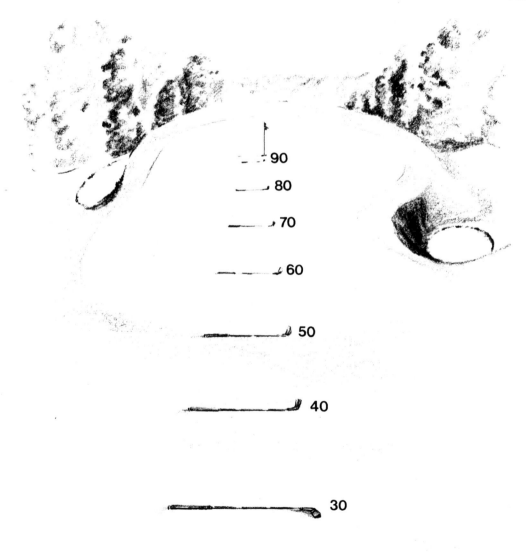

A 'ladder' of clubs for practising long pitching

the shot not only by eye but by knowing the precise length required. A set of five or six coloured hoops at specific distances gives an excellent way of practising shots of different lengths, again pacing the distances out and setting the targets at set lengths.

A pitching routine

As with the long game it is good to have a definite routine for playing shots. It is all too easy for players to practise pitching on a practice ground by looking at the ball, looking up once and making a quick judgement. On the golf course they then often do something completely different, looking at the target three or four times. On a practice ground they are making a quick and spontaneous judgement, but on the course tend to slow down and look at things quite differently. Often judgement on a practice ground is far more accurate than with the deliberate approach they adopt on the course. With both short pitching and long pitching it is good to have a routine. With short pitching this probably means two practice swings to feel the depth of contact, with the long pitch perhaps just one small loosening-up movement, combined with looking up and judging the distance in a specific way, two looks almost certainly being sufficient to make an accurate, unmuddled assessment of length.

The cut-up shot

It is fairly seldom that you need a cut-up shot around the green. The object of the shot is not so much getting backspin and stop, as the club golfer imagines, but more getting height to get over an obstacle. To practise cut-up shots try to find an area with comparatively thick grass and a small tree which you can use as your obstacle. Open the clubface wide, feeling that it lies on its back, and practise sliding the clubhead beneath the ball until the ball pops up quickly. Gradually try to move closer and closer to the tree until the ball can come up almost vertically. It is a good competitive practice at the end of a training session for players to see just who can get closest to the tree and still get

the ball up and over it. Good juniors can often develop clubhead control by learning to open the clubface on a 7 or 8-iron and produce the same kind of shot, giving them an insight into just what you can do with the various clubs in the bag – practice rather than a shot for actual use.

A cut-up and catch shot

Learning to open the clubface well with a sand wedge is essential when coming onto bunker shots. An exercise which usually appeals to youngsters is to sit the ball up on a reasonably thick piece of grass, to open the clubface with a sand wedge and to try to pop the ball up quickly and then catch it in midair. Obviously the shot as such is useless but it does help give young players the feeling of being able to keep the clubface open and produce tremendous backspin, a feeling they will need in certain situations, particularly in a bunker. The feeling is that the clubhead lies right on its back; the feet are turned very much to the left to bring the clubface to aim on target, sliding the clubhead beneath the ball, with the left elbow then drawing away behind the player in the through-swing as the clubface comes through in its very open-faced position. The shot is only possible with the ball sitting really well.

Competitive Pitching Practices

Good young players often have a real weakness with their short game. Competitive practices are usually the answer to teaching them the shortcomings in their own game and then producing a short game which works under pressure.

Pitching to a £5 note

A good training exercise with ten or twelve players is to get them all to put money in a kitty, producing from this a £5 note which then can be pinned to a green, preferably just over a small bunker and within 10 yards of where the shots are going to be played. The players take it in turns to have one shot at the £5 note, the idea being to land on it (not staying on it). Players take one shot at a time, with, say, five rounds. The first player (or players in each round) to land on the note wins the money. If several players in one round land on it, the prize is split. The task usually proves impossible. The main difficulty is that most players are so eager to look up to see whether they have won the money that they in fact fluff the shot. This can then be developed by putting players into pairs where one player plays the shot and the other watches to be ready to claim the prize. Players are then able to see how much better they do when they stay looking down, and trust their partner to monitor the result. This can be adapted as a junior competition according to age and ability by using a small metal bar tray or some other flat object.

Pitching to an umbrella

Another competitive practice is for players to have a specified number of balls to pitch into an umbrella, say, 10 yards, 20 yards or 30 yards away; the player getting most in wins. This can be varied by setting out targets of different sizes at the same distance, something between 10 and 15 yards apart. An open umbrella is one target, a hoop the second and a smallish tyre the third. The player has, say, twenty balls and scores one point for the umbrella, two for the hoop and three for the tyre – having a completely free choice of which target to aim for.

Long pitching

A competitive long-pitching exercise is to set out five umbrellas at different distances, 30 yards, 40 yards and up to 70 yards. These can be used by about six to eight players in a slight V formation so that the distances are roughly equal for each. Players start by aiming at the 30-yard umbrella and go on hitting balls until they pitch one in that. They move on to the 40-yard umbrella and, having pitched into that, move on to the 50 yards and so on. Each should be given a specified number of balls to start

with, say sixty, the one reaching the last umbrella and landing in that in the fewest shots being the winner. By having a specified number of balls there is then always a check on how many balls each player has used. Again this can be varied to make it easier or more difficult according to the number of players, their standard and the time allotted for the practice.

A pitching competition

An ideal way of practising pitching is to have a closely mown area with a flag in it, marking off circles around the flag at two yards, five yards and 10 yards. Players can then practise pitching to this, counting the number of shots finishing within each zone. This provides a good way of having a competitive session, preferably hitting shots to this target from different distances. An ideal competition is to give players twenty shots from five different spots, scoring ten points for a ball going in the hole, six for the closest ring, three for the next ring and one for the outside ring. This can be adapted as a team competition.

Pitch and putt as a competitive short-pitching exercise over a bunker

Emphasis can be put on getting down in a pitch and one putt. One way of doing this is to give the player six balls to hit from behind a bunker, with a shot of say 10 yards, counting the total number of shots to get these balls down the hole. This puts emphasis on getting the ball close and on good holing-out. Again this can be played as a head-to-head singles game, as a competitive practice on your own, or with teams of players all doing the same task.

A variation of this, particularly for good players, is for each player to take it in turns to play a specific shot from behind a bunker, the idea being to do the most consecutive shots getting up and down in a pitch and a putt. The first player goes on until he fails to get up and down in two and the winner is the one who has the most consecutive one putts. If there is a tie they can have a sudden-death play-off or have one shot at the flag, the closest to the hole winning.

Bunker Shots – General Technique

The splash shot from a good lie in a bunker round a green should cause very little trouble but gives no end of difficulty to most club golfers. The idea of the splash shot is literally to splash out a handful of sand and make the ball pop out with the sand. To make this as easy as possible the clubhead should be positioned an inch or so behind the ball. The eyes are focused on a spot in the sand just behind the ball, never looking at the ball itself. One of the main difficulties for the club golfer is in opening the clubface at address and through impact to keep sufficient loft on the club. The more lofted the sand iron you possess, the easier the shot will be and the less you have to open the clubface. The clubface should be opened to increase the loft before the club is gripped, ensuring that the right hand is always behind the club and not underneath it in an attempt to scoop the ball upwards. Having opened the clubface, make sure the ball is still towards the middle to toe of the club and not brought towards the socket. At this point the clubface will be facing away to the right of the line of your feet. Turn the whole clubhead and your feet round to the left until the bottom groove on the clubface aims at your target. The ball should be played well forward in the feet, feeling opposite your left eye or left ear. Swing the club back and through virtually on a straight line from the flag to the ball, cocking the wrists in the backswing but then definitely holding the clubface open through impact, allowing the left elbow to draw back behind you in the through-swing so that the clubface is held open. The left hand and wrist need to be firmly in control, never having any feeling of flicking the club-head through with the right hand and wrist. The end of the swing should be a fairly full one, weight moving well through onto the left foot.

In the whole shot the eyes are kept focused on the sand behind the ball, not just digging the clubhead into the sand but splashing through and out the other side. By practising with an open clubface on thick grass the player can usually get the feeling of how the clubface should move through impact and the added backspin it gives to the shot.

Basic Bunker Shot Practices

Drawing a circle

The feeling with a splash shot should be one of splashing out a circle of sand with the ball in the middle of it. A good way for the long-handicapped player to practise is by drawing a circle in the sand around the ball from say an inch and a half behind it to an inch and a half in front. Try to splash out the circle of sand and the ball will come out with it. A way of developing really good control for taking the sand is to draw a line of little circles or oval marks in the sand, taking practice swings and simply splashing through the sand until this can be done quite accurately. You can then put a ball in the middle of the last circle, splashing away the sand and finding that the ball comes out with it. Once you have this feeling you can develop it further by simply marking a spot in the sand behind the ball and concentrating on that, eventually finding that you can choose a spot in the sand and watch that to the same effect, without of course touching or marking the sand.

A perfect contact

The worst error in bunker shots is hitting the ball from the socket. Many players shank (socket) their bunker shots by opening the clubface, keeping the ball too near the socket and swinging excessively out to in across the body. The feeling with a bunker shot should be one of turning the stance to the left to bring the clubface on target and then simply swinging straight back and through on this path. Many

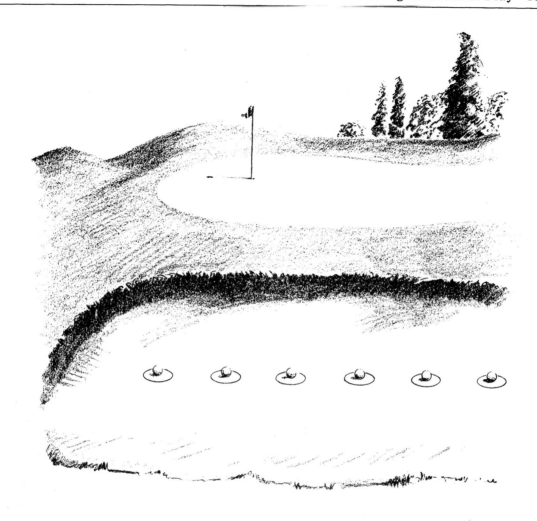

Learning bunker shots by marking circles round the ball

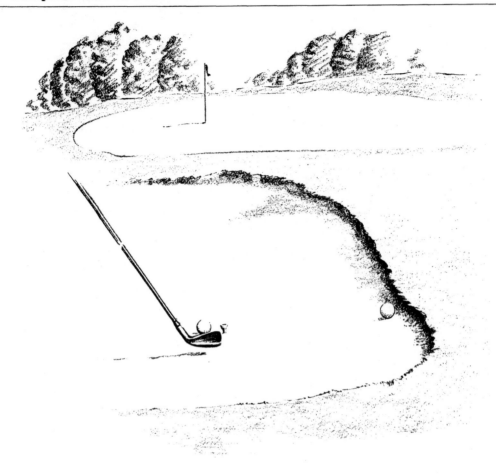

Curing a shank in the bunker – striking the ball and leaving the tee in place

players who socket the ball in a bunker imagine they are topping it. To check this, set your clubface to a ball and put a tee peg an inch outside the ball. Keep the ball if anything towards the toe of the club and practise shots, ensuring that you don't hit the tee peg as well. Similarly, with safety in mind and providing you have plenty of space, you can put down two balls in the bunker an inch apart, concentrating on hitting the inside one without touching the outside one. Again, if you tend to catch both, the odds are you are opening the clubface and pushing the ball towards the socket or swinging excessively out to in. In this way you can check for a perfect contact and ensure you really are hitting the ball from the middle of the clubface.

Practice Routines

The 12-yard bunker shot

A good general-purpose distance for a splash shot round the green is a 12-yard shot. This should be long enough to get out of most bunkers and onto the green without being so long that it is likely to go through the other side. Practise one set distance and you can then get the idea of varying this distance up and downwards. A good way of practising bunker shots is to measure out this distance of 12 yards and to put a target at that point on the green, whether a pitch-mark repairer or, if you have one, a plastic hoop to try and land in. Alternatively, if you don't have a green to practise to, measure out 12 yards and again put down a hoop or your practice-ball bag as a target. Don't simply aim to the flag on your practice green if this is an unsuitable distance from you.

A good player's practice

One of the best ways of practising bunker shots is to put a hoop out on a green at the set distance of 12 yards. Practise hitting bunker shots until you feel you can reliably land the ball in the hoop or very near to it. Use groups of 10 balls and monitor your success rate until you can get a higher and higher proportion of shots in the hoop.

Monitoring your bunker shots

If anything, most people who play reasonably good bunker shots will tend to leave the shot short of the target and possibly allow it to drift too far to the right. If you have a flag to play to at a suitable distance of between 10 and 15 yards, monitor your bunker shots carefully by seeing just how many of them do land short and to the right. A good way for the aspiring top-class player to practise these shots is to monitor his records on a piece of paper marked with circles with a dot in the middle of each circle which represents the flag. Play groups of ten shots and then plot out the pattern of these results until you get a picture of your own grouping and positioning. Keep on doing this until

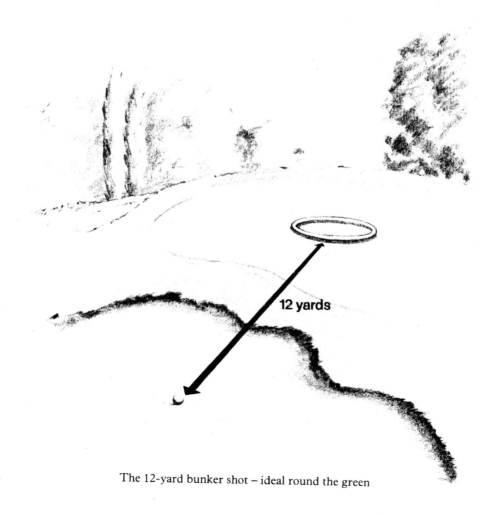

12 yards

The 12-yard bunker shot – ideal round the green

the pattern shows the shots are fairly evenly spread. It is very easy to get into a pattern where you are consistently short or consistently to the right with bunker shots without realizing it and therefore without working on it.

Varying distances

The 12-yard bunker shot is a good general-purpose splash shot. Most club golfers try to vary distance too much before they can produce one set length. Once you can produce reliable shots of one length, try to vary these upwards or downwards, first starting off with a shot of about eight yards and another, longer one of say 20 yards. The shorter shot is as a rule the more difficult, requiring a slower, smaller version of the ordinary splash shot, possibly trying to take just a little more sand. The danger for the club player in slowing down the swing is that he decelerates and loses speed altogether. It is therefore a fairly advanced shot and the long-handicapped player often does best to stick with his ordinary-length shot and to be satisfied to be a few feet past the flag. To produce the longer shot of about 20 yards, play much the same splash shot as for 12 yards but with the clubface squared up instead of open. This should produce less loft and therefore a little more length. Again, in doing these shots, an ideal way of practising the three distances is to put out three hoops, one at eight yards, one at 12 yards and one at 20 yards, to get a real feel for the distances.

Perfecting the splash shot

An excellent way for the top-class player to practise bunker shots is to set out a row of clubs in front of him at two-yard intervals, at 7 yards, 9 yards, 11 yards and so on up to 21 yards. He can practise pitching the ball between the first two clubs, the second two and so on. He can then motivate himself to see how few shots he needs to execute this ladder, counting how many shots it takes him to get between the first two clubs, then moving on to the second and counting the shots needed to negotiate this and

so on until the last target is completed. This too can be adapted as a competitive practice for the end of a practice session for top-class players.

Getting up and down

The aim for the good player in playing a bunker shot round the green is to get up and down in two, perhaps even holing the occasional shot. A good way of practising which teaches the player to take time and care over each shot is to hit the shot and then go forward and putt out. The player can get some very solid practice by playing ten bunker shots, putting out with each and seeing just how many it takes him to hole out all ten shots. He can then give himself a target, trying to improve on this target until he achieves the ultimate of getting down in twenty or less. This again begins to simulate the pressure of tournament golf and to make each shot really count. This too can be done as a competitive practice in a training session, players tackling the task one at a time and carefully recording their scores.

Competitive practice

A simple competitive practice is for players to be given ten balls to splash out and land in a hoop, the one getting the most to land in the hoop (not necessarily staying there) being the winner.

A head-to-head practice

A good team practice is for players to be paired off against each other and to be given two identical bunker shots to play. The one getting closer to the hole with each shot wins a point for his team. On a simple head-to-head basis between two players they can take it in turns to choose a spot to play from, the closer to the hole winning each round. Alternatively they can play a match from a bunker of eighteen holes, choosing in turn the spot they play from, playing the bunker shot and then holing out with as many putts as are necessary, scoring the match in the same way as an ordinary round of golf.

A buried ball. With the ball buried or in a footprint
the shot played is an explosion shot, blasting out
the ball and sand with a downward attack. The ball
is positioned centrally in the stance, clubface square
or slightly closed, weight on the left foot and hands
ahead of the ball. The club is then lifted fairly
sharply in the backswing and with the eyes focused
just behind the ball the clubhead blasts down and
through the sand, forcing out the ball

Approach pitching. In the long pitch shot played with a 9-iron, pitching wedge or sand wedge, the ball is played behind the centre of the stance to encourage a descending blow. The hands are held slightly ahead of the ball, weight favouring the left foot, most players finding it necessary to turn the feet and knees to the left while keeping the shoulders square, to keep the ball travelling on target. Hands and wrists are down and forward at address, giving an in-built wrist cock. This is added to slightly on the backswing, the left hand very firmly in control. In the throughswing weight is very definitely transferred onto the left foot, punching through into a strong finish, where the back of the left wrist leads. The finish is firm but with the left upper arm still staying well into the body, the feet and legs being active. Stress must be put on accelerating through the ball

The short pitch. In a short pitch from a good lie
where the whole ball sits above the ground, the shot
is played with a sand wedge, arms hanging close to
the side, wrists firm, hands level and not ahead of
the ball, giving a maximum loft to the club. The feet
can be turned out slightly, the action then being
one of moving the club back and through with no
wrist action, elbows and upper arms kept tucked
into the side and the feet and legs working actively
through the ball. Only where the ball sits very
poorly is wrist action needed. In that case the long
pitch action is reduced in length and speed to nip
the ball away – a very advanced shot

The splash shot. The splash shot is played from a good lie around the green at perhaps 10 to 20 yards. The clubface is held open before gripping the club, keeping the right palm behind and not beneath the shaft. The clubhead is positioned about an inch behind the ball, the eyes focused on a spot just ahead of this and behind the ball. With the clubface open the whole stance has to be turned to the left until the clubface in its open position aims at the target. The ball is played well forward in the stance, the swing being very full and slow, cocking the wrists in the backswing but using firm wrists through impact so that the clubface is held open, splashing the ball out gently but going through to a full finish, weight on the left foot (sequence: Peter Jacobsen)

From beneath the face. With the ball in the face of
a bunker, stand well up the bank, leaning into it.
The clubface is held squarely, looking at the back
of the ball and chopping directly into it. The ball
is then forced up and out, the weight leaning into
the bank throughout

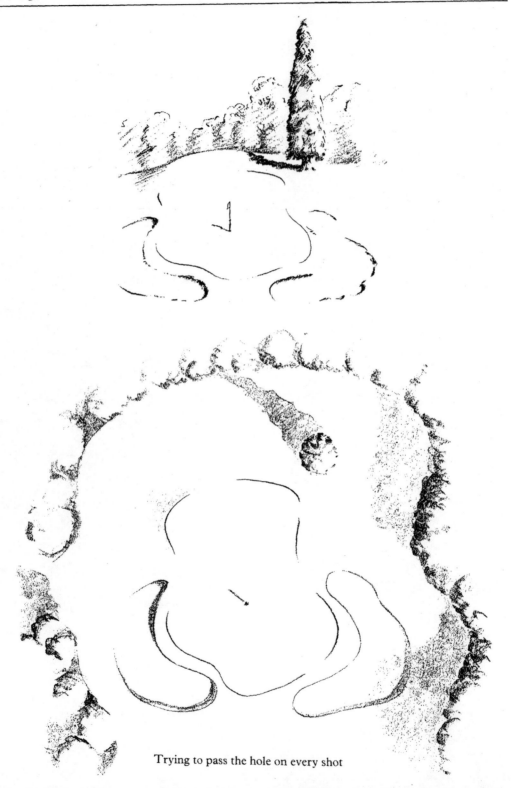

Trying to pass the hole on every shot

6 Practice on the Course

Many players get a lot of benefit from being able to play a few holes on their own, possibly hitting two or three balls to the green or from the tee and being able to practise extra short game shots. Unfortunately, but understandably, this isn't always allowed on golf courses, which become ever more crowded. But for the good player there is little to compare with being able to hit extra shots from bunkers or extra little chips around the green to get the feel for the short game. Even without being able to play extra balls, however, there are many ways in which you can practise on the golf course, either playing on your own or with other people, to prepare yourself for competitive play. Here are six ideas for making your friendly games of golf more interesting and for ideas to work at to improve your own standard of play.

Passing the Flag

One of the main failures of most golfers, particularly the ordinary club golfer, is in continually being short of the flag. On most golf courses the main areas of trouble are likely to be short of the green, possibly with a bunker both right and left short of almost every green on the course. Players frequently underclub. An excellent way of practising, particularly in the autumn and winter when the greens are holding, is to attempt to hit every ball to the green so that it passes the flag, the idea being to be beyond the flag but on the green with every shot. Analyse this on the card, giving yourself a tick every time you pass the flag with your shot to the green, with two ticks if it is actually on the green and past the flag. In this way you may well find a definite weakness in your game of not being sufficiently bold and attacking but consistently underclubbing.

Analysing Your Round

Many golfers of a comparatively high standard do not realize the weaknesses in their game. Very often they will be consistently off the fairway on one side or the other with their drives, possibly far too often short with their second shots, and may have a particular weakness with chipping or putting of which they are not always aware. Often, for example, you will find a player who thinks that he hooks the ball off the tee and yet he misses far more fairways on the right. Other players consistently pitch or chip several feet short of the flag and again may not realize how many shots this costs them. The good player, or anyone aspiring to play good golf, should spend time analysing each round of golf to see where errors creep in. I would suggest marking the card and analysing the round of golf in the following way. Set out the columns marked for drives, shots to the green, and putts. Look at your drives and give yourself a tick if you hit the fairway, two ticks if you hit a virtually perfect drive in the correct position. If you miss the fairway, put a cross and an R or L to indicate which side you have missed it on. With the second shot, or any shot to the green, which may be a second shot on a par five, give yourself a tick if you hit the green and then mark how many feet you are past the flag or short of the flag. For example, + 20 is

20 feet past the flag, and −8 is 8 feet short. Be realistic about the distances, working in feet, yards or metres if you prefer. For the good player it is also worth noting whether the ball is very far right or left on the green. If you miss the green, put a cross and mark whether you are short left (SL), short right (SR), past left (PL), or past right (PR). If you leave yourself a chip or a putt or a bunker shot, make a note in the margin of how close you get with this, e.g. BS10 (a bunker shot to 10 feet), C-5 (a chip shot 5 feet short), P + 12 (a pitch 12 feet past), then keep a note of the number of putts and the distance of the putts. For example, you may find yourself having taken three putts from 11 yards with the first putt finishing four feet short. In this way it should become apparent if you make any particular error. Although one may imagine that players are aware of their own shortcomings, this often is not the case, particularly with faults such as underclubbing or missing greens consistently on one particular side.

Attacking with the Short Game

Players will often be as consistently tentative with their short game as they are with their long game, constantly leaving the ball short of the flag with every chip, pitch or long putt. Attempt to play a round of golf with every single shot to the flag passing the flag. Again this is of particular benefit in the autumn and winter months when the greens are holding well. In a game of golf, have a side bet with your opponent, paying a small fine every time you are short of the flag with the chip, long putt, pitch or bunker shot. You should soon find yourself attacking the flag in a far more aggressive manner, beginning to judge distance around the flag more accurately.

Nominating the Target

An excellent discipline for the good golfer is to be really specific about aiming to a target. All shots should of course be aimed at a specific point but it is very easy in driving, in particular, simply to look at the obstacles to the side of the fairway and to think of threading the ball between these. Correctly you should always choose a target, both for direction and distance, and aim at landing the ball at this. For a good player, an excellent exercise is to tell his partner or opponent precisely where he is aiming the ball and precisely what he is intending to do with it. This focuses his attention on what he is doing and doesn't allow him to hit a slightly offline shot and pretend it was what he meant to do. The player should state quite firmly where he intends to hit the ball and, if he is of a very high standard, nominate whether he expects it to bend slightly left to right or slightly right to left. In the same way with a bunker shot, with chipping, pitching and putting he should state firmly his objectives and nominate the line. He should also in stating his intentions on reading greens, particularly with long putts, get his marker or opponent to monitor his reading of the greens. He should say where he intends to start the ball on a long putt with someone else pointing out to him whether or not the putt starts on line. Frequently players will choose a line with a long putt and then not start the ball off correctly. The feedback they receive is often muddled, and they don't know whether they have started the ball wrongly or misread the putt.

Varying Second Shots

Frequently players who play on ordinary club courses get insufficient practice for tournaments. The good golfer will often find it beneficial to play a round of golf where he gives himself a variety of long second shots, either using a 4-iron off every tee, preferably without a peg, to practice his long irons and then making the second shots far more testing, or by hitting his drives but then playing the second shot to give himself a wood, 4-iron or 3-iron for every shot into the green. In this way he can make the course as demanding as he wants and can transform even the most ordinary golf course

Nominating the shots to focus your mind

into one which is comparatively challenging. This is particularly helpful if he knows well the distances from certain landmarks on the course, planning beforehand where he intends hitting his second shots.

Monitoring Success

A way for players to have a scoring system in a practice or training session is to devise a points system which makes each shot important, while giving the players flexibility to work on any changes in technique. A system is to score one point for each of the following achievements:

1. Hitting the drive on the fairway.
2. Hitting the green with the first shot which can reach the green.
3. An extra point if that ball finishes on the green past the flag.
4. For chipping in.
5. For getting up and down in two from a bunker.
6. For a single putt.

7. For a birdie (or three for a birdie, two for a par and one for one over – according to standard).

In this way the player always has a chance of scoring points, while putting a premium on good driving, aggressive iron play, chipping and bunker shots.

Laybacks

As explained in the section on putting, a good nine-hole challenge match is to make short putting more difficult and to practise short putting ready for a tournament situation. In this game any putt after the first putt is lengthened by one club length so that you keep facing telling short putts. In other words, if your first putt finishes eight inches away you have to pull it a further length back. If you then miss that putt and move it say one foot away you again have to move that back a putter length. This puts emphasis on getting the long putt really close and on good holing-out.

Standing above the ball. In standing above the ball the feet will necessarily move closer to the ball, the body bent over more than on a flat lie. This produces a very upright plane to the swing, tending to send the ball slicing away to the right. The key point is to keep very good balance, resisting any tendency to fall forwards onto the ball, watching the ball well through impact. The player then needs to aim very well to the left of the target, allowing for the ball to bend severely right in the air and possibly to bounce further right on landing

Standing below the ball. In standing below the ball the feet are going to be further from the ball than normal, the player standing in a more upright position, which produces a flattish swing round the body. This will often bring out the best in the club golfer's swing, producing a shot which tends to bend away to the left. The club can be gripped an inch or so further down the shaft than normal, aiming well away to the right to allow for the ball to bend in the air and kick further left on landing

Right The downhill shot. In playing downhill, the effective loft of the club is always reduced so that the ball tends to fly off low. The main difficulty is in striking the ball cleanly without touching any ground behind it. To make this as easy as possible the ball should be played back in the stance, well towards the right foot, keeping the weight on the left foot so that the body almost stands out at right angles to the slope. The hands will be ahead of the ball, clubface tipped over, thus reducing the loft. In this case a 6-iron may fly off with a loft of about a 3-iron so that a shorter club than normal is chosen. The ball will if anything also tend to push away to the right, so that the feet have to be aimed left of target to allow for this

An uphill shot. In playing from an uphill lie, the feeling should be of leaning into the bank so that the weight is kept on the left foot while maintaining balance throughout. The swing should be executed virtually the same way as normally, really making sure that the weight does move onto the left foot through and beyond impact. If there is any tendency to fall back, the shot tends to be pulled away to the left. If the player overdoes the movement through onto the left, the ball may in fact be pushed to the right. Balance is the key to playing these shots well

The downhill pitch. A downhill pitch shot of perhaps 10–12 yards from a downhill bank over a bunker should be played with a sand wedge, playing the ball well back in the feet, keeping the weight towards the left foot while maintaining balance, keeping the right shoulder as high as possible. This makes it as easy as you can to get the club up and down the bank, resisting any tendency to help the ball into the air. The clubhead should feel as if it is sliding down the bank beyond impact, keeping good balance throughout. The downhill bunker shot is tackled in the same way, weight on the left foot, shoulders following the slope of the ground and again with the feeling of swinging up the bank in the backswing and then down the bank beyond impact

Playing up a bank. The easiest way of playing a shot up and over a bank is to use a putter so that the ball runs up the bank and trickles over the other side. Only if the grass is thick and the ball unlikely to run through it should the bank be negotiated with a wedge

A punch shot. A punch shot with a long or medium iron is played in much the same way as a long pitch. The ball is played back in the feet, the hands ahead to reduce the effect of loft of the club. The weight is kept on the left foot throughout, cocking the wrists slightly in the backswing with the left hand very much in control and then moving through onto the left foot with a firm, punchy finish, again the back of the left wrist leading. The shot is used either as a low recovery shot when trees impede the normal route to the hole or to keep the ball low when playing into the wind (sequence: Lee Trevino)

7 Fitness for Golf

Golf, like any other sport, requires a certain degree of fitness to play the game well. It does after all involve walking between three and four miles for each round, not necessarily on flat ground, possibly carrying a fairly hefty bag of golf clubs, and hitting a ball long distances. The top-class player needs to be exceptionally fit, able to play as many as thirty-six holes a day over four or five days in county matches or international matches. The legs need to be strong to walk the course without tiring, you need stamina, both physical and mental, to be as fresh on the last two or three holes of the round as at the beginning. The hands, wrists, arms, legs and back need to be strong, with considerable flexibility in the limbs and body. Many problems encountered by club players are from lack of flexibility and often from being unsatisfactorily right-hand dominant. For the top-class golfer there must be considerable emphasis placed on fitness, combined with a sound energy-giving diet. A good diet for golfers should provide energy to sustain the player for anything up to five hours – with an added intake of some sort of food and most definitely some liquid during the round. For players in relatively cool climates this is almost as important as in hot weather. The body needs fuel on which to function; many players lose concentration or suffer tiredness in the closing holes and this is fairly easily rectified with some sort of nourishment.

The exercises that follow have been divided into sections. Most can be adapted by increasing the numbers of repetitions performed, giving ideas for everyone from the non-athletic middle-aged club golfer to the aspiring champion. Those exercises marked *** are particularly recommended for top-class players. None of the exercises require any special equipment, apart from dumbbells for forearm and wrist exercises. Good luck.

Golfing Exercises

★★★ Left armswings

Hold the club in your left hand, possibly with the thumb slightly more down the grip than normal. Swing the club up to the top of the backswing, supporting it on the left thumb, and then swing the club through, again supporting it on the left thumb at the end of the swing, the arm folding into a virtual right angle as it would with both hands. The arm must not be kept straight beyond the bottom of the swing, firstly because it is not what is wanted in the swing itself and secondly because it can damage the shoulder. From the end of the swing, lower the club slowly to address and begin again. This can help strengthen the left arm to match the strength of the right and also encourages the left arm to fold in correctly. A 6-iron is an ideal club for the left-arm exercises. The good player can develop these further by using a specially weighted club.

Left arm bounces

Grip the club with the left hand alone and swing up to the top of the backswing by supporting the club on the left thumb. From here bounce the club up and down ten times and then return it to address slowly. Repeat this. Initially ten bounces may be too many for the club golfer but gradually the movement should be built up to this number. This encourages the left hand and arm to stay in control during the change of directions at the top of the swing, allowing the right hand and arm to be less dominant.

Left wrist twists

Hold the club in the left hand and swing it slowly from address to the top of the backswing, supporting it on the left thumb. Now roll the left wrist over and back, feeling the back of the left wrist gaining strength. Start by doing this five times and then lower the club to address, repeating this and building up the number of wrist twists as the arm and wrist get stronger.

Continuous swinging

Hold your 6-iron with an ordinary grip and swing the club fast and furiously, back and through, back and through, through a comparatively short distance, clubhead going no more than shoulder height, with emphasis on turning the forearms and whipping the clubhead through at speed with the wrists and forearms.

This encourages the club golfer to use his hands and wrists properly, strengthening them while developing looseness. For women it is particularly helpful in developing the 'suddenness' at the bottom of the swing which is required to generate clubhead speed.

Left wrist twists

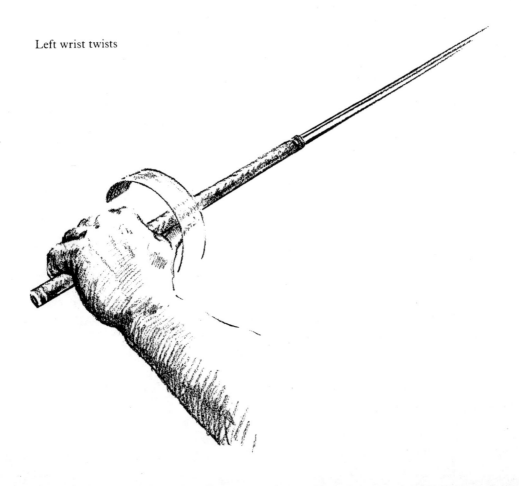

Grass-cutting

The continuous swinging exercise above can be developed further for strengthening the hands and wrists by swinging the club back and through, back and through in some fairly thick but short rough. This again requires speed and control in the wrists and forearms. The shorter the swing is kept, the more the hands and wrists will have to work.

Swinging three clubs

Swinging a weighted club or swinging three clubs is a good general exercise both for loosening up and for strengthening the muscles. It is *not* to be recommended as a loosening-up exercise just before playing, for it tends to take away the feel for swinging one club. It is,

however, a very good exercise on a practice ground or in the garden. It is also a good exercise for the player who has difficulty in keeping the swing slow and smooth, building up the feeling of rhythm and control. As a teaching aid it can be particularly helpful in trying to teach players the necessary slow timing for short pitches and bunker shots.

*** Hitting a row of ten balls

This is an exercise particularly good for the aspiring top-class player. Line up a row of ten balls and hit this row of balls one by one with a 5-iron. Set the balls about four inches apart, address each in the normal way, swing through to a sound finish but then return almost immediately and step forward and hit the next. The ball should be hit as hard as possible, with

Overheads

emphasis on good balance, watching each ball, and particularly on breathing correctly and recovering between shots. This is a general strengthening exercise, particularly useful for good youngsters.

Warming Up

The golfer should warm up before any practice session or before going on the golf course in the same way as any other athlete. These exercises are general warming-up exercises, some or all of which will give a good preparation for practice or play.

Neck loosening

Starting at the top, move your head slowly over to the right and then over to the left as though putting the right ear on the right shoulder and then the left ear on the left shoulder. Then let the head fall forwards and backwards and finally round and round a few times, backwards, down to the left, down in front and down to the right. Particularly in the older golfer this freedom in the neck is essential in golf to allow the body and shoulders to turn while the head stays still, eyes focused on the ball.

★★★ Overheads

Hold your driver in front of you, arms straight, left hand at the top of the grip and right hand down by the head of the club. Bring the club back over your head, preferably keeping the arms straight, and then bring it back again to the starting point. The looser and freer your shoulders, the shorter the club you can use for this exercise. Some players will find it difficult with a club the length of the driver, others can do the same with a wedge or even a putter. Try this as an initial loosening exercise on the practice ground or in the garden. Do not attempt it before going out to play in a match in case your shoulders aren't as supple as you imagine!

Club twists

Club twists

To loosen up your back, hold a club behind your back, passing your arms over the club so that it is held between both elbows in the back. Put your feet apart as in the ordinary address position and simply turn to the right, twisting in the body and then turn to the left. Ease yourself gradually round as far as you can turn, without bouncing or trying to force yourself further than you can manage. This exercise will loosen up the muscles in the trunk and lower back.

Passing the ball

Hold both arms out in front of you at almost shoulder height, a golf ball in one hand. Now swing both arms round behind you, still keeping the arms straight, and pass the ball from one hand to the other behind your back.

Passing the ball

Providing your arms and shoulders are flexible the exercise should be comparatively simple, gradually loosening the arms so that they move freely from the shoulders.

A figure of eight

Put your feet approximately 18 inches apart. Bend over and hold a golf ball in your right hand by your right ankle. Now simply pass the ball in front of your right leg and transfer the ball into your left hand behind your left leg. Take the ball around the front of your left leg, pass it behind your right leg and transfer the ball into your right hand. Continue this for about ten repetitions. It is simply an exercise to loosen up the back, to get the arms moving and to get you focusing your attention on the golf ball!

Figure of eight

Cross-over stretches

Stand with your feet approximately two feet apart and bend and twist, to touch your left foot with your right finger tips, left arm stretching up behind you. Then bring the left arm down to touch the right toes with the left fingers, right arm extended up behind you. Keep the legs as straight as possible throughout, bouncing gently from side to side, again to loosen up the back and to get the arms swinging freely from the shoulders.

Sideways trunk bends

The back and body have to twist in the golf swing. A good loosening-up exercise is to stand with your feet approximately two feet apart. Bending not forward but straight over to the side, ease your right hand as far down the side of your right leg as you can and then come up into an upright position and repeat this by bending over to the left and stretching the left hand as far as possible down the left leg. Cor-

rectly this should be done by simply easing the hand down the leg and not by trying to bounce the hand up and down. A bouncing movement can often stretch the body just a little further than it wants to go. Ease the hand gently down the leg, gradually building up more freedom.

Leg lunges

The legs and ankles need strengthening and also loosening up to perform well and to cope with walking on the course. Stand with your right foot pointing directly in front of you and your left foot out behind you, so that the feet form a parallel line beneath your body, the right heel and the left toes approximately two feet apart. Bend the right knee, pressing down on the right knee with the hands while keeping the left heel firmly on the ground. Just adopt this position, staying in it for a minute or so, feeling the stretch in the left leg. This should *not* be done with any form of bouncing action but is a stationary position which stretches and tones the muscles in the back of the left leg. Change

18"

Leg lunges

position and do the same with the right foot out behind. Ensure, for maximum benefit, that the back heel is kept down on the ground, adjusting the distance between your feet if necessary to make this possible. Keep the feet parallel and pointing straight in front of you.

General Mobility

Good golfers as a rule have a very high degree of flexibility in the shoulders, legs, hands and wrists. Frequently the club golfer does not appreciate the degree of movement that the professional golfer is usually able to achieve. The club golfer will often find difficulty in producing a perfectly orthodox golf swing because of lack of flexibility in some part of the body. He may try to do things which his body simply is not capable of doing. These exercises, while useful for the good golfer, are essential for the club player and particularly for the older golfer.

Finger separations

Good golf depends on having strong hands and supple fingers. Frequently the club golfer has difficulty with the grip and hand action because his fingers are stiff. To loosen the fingers, put both hands out in front of you, palms of the hands facing downwards. Spread the hands right out so that the fingers and thumbs form as wide a spread as possible. Now close the hands up in front of you and spread them out again, this time keeping the middle two fingers of each hand together and opening wide the index fingers, little fingers and thumbs. This right-hand spread is the one you need in the grip. Now close the hands up together again and this time spread them apart, keeping first and second fingers together, third and fourth fingers together. Keep repeating this, out and in, out and in as wide as possible. Many people do not have this degree of control of the fingers and will often find that their hands seem to have minds of their own. The exercise not only develops flexibility to encourage a good grip but is also generally strengthening for the whole hand and fingers.

Wrist stretches

The club golfer often finds the golf swing difficult because he cannot bend his wrists freely backwards and forwards to form right angles with the forearms. Practise easing the hands and wrists forward by holding the thumb of one hand and pulling the hand forward to bring that thumb down onto the forearm. If the wrists are free and easy the thumbs can probably be eased down onto the forearms. If not, working at this over a period of time should loosen the wrists and, as the player gets older, will keep the wrists mobile. To check the backward movements of the wrists, hold both arms out in front of you at shoulder height, putting the palms of the hands flat against a wall. If the wrists are free and loose you should be able to form an easy right angle between your arms and the wall. Gradually let your hands creep slightly down the wall, the palms remaining flat against the wall, making the angle sharper than a right angle.

Overheads – shortening the club

Hold a driver in front of you, left hand at the top of the grip and right hand at the head of the club. Now with the arms straight take the club back over your head and down behind you and then bring it back again. The arms should be kept straight throughout. This exercise loosens up the arms and keeps them swinging freely from the shoulders. Gradually develop this until you can do it with a shorter club, moving on as you improve from the woods through to the shortest irons. This helps the arms to move as freely as possible from the body, encouraging a fluent swing where the two can work almost independently.

Wall touches

Stand with your feet approximately 18 inches apart with the backs of your heels approximately 12–15 inches from a wall. With your feet firmly anchored to the ground, turn and put the palms of both hands flat on the wall at roughly shoulder level. Now turn the other way, still

Wall touches

keeping both feet flat on the ground, and once more put the palms of the hands on the wall. Keep repeating this to loosen the pelvis and back.

Left arm presses

To produce a good backswing the left arm needs to swing the club up towards the right shoulder. The good golfer draws the left arm close across the chest; the closer it comes to the right shoulder, the straighter the left arm will stay. As an exercise, stand upright and hold your left arm in front of you at shoulder level, palm downwards. Clasp the left elbow with your right hand and pull the left arm across your body towards your right shoulder. The golfer who is really loose in the left shoulder can draw the arm across to touch the right shoulder quite easily. Many club golfers and middle-aged players find this extremely difficult and need to compensate for this lack of flexibility in the way they swing. Gradually learn to ease the arm across the chest and then develop the exercise further by swinging the left arm across to the right shoulder as tight as possible without the right hand helping.

Brushing floor and ceiling

This is a general mobility exercise to get the whole body working freely. Stand with your feet approximately 18 inches apart, legs straight, and hang the arms down in front of you. Feel that your fingertips brush the ground from left to right and then stretch upwards, as though trying to brush the ceiling with your fingertips. Continue the circle on through, bending to brush the floor and then stretching as though brushing the ceiling, doing this several times in one direction and then turning and changing directions.

Left leg and ankle twists

The left leg and ankle need considerable freedom in the golf swing. By the time you finish the swing the left foot should still be pointing more or less straight in front of you while the hips have to turn to face the target. Developing this freedom is essential for a sound swing. Stand with your feet approximately 12 inches apart, toes turned perhaps 10 degrees inwards, hands resting on the back of a chair. Now twist from the left ankle and knee upwards, until your hips face directly left, right foot up on its toes so that the knees touch. Feel that the left leg is able to straighten and keep repeating this exercise until the movement becomes easy and the ankle and leg can twist.

Left leg twists

Arms and Wrists

Finger stretches

Hold your arms out at full stretch at around shoulder height. Now stretch and push the fingers out in front of you as far and wide as they will go and then pull them in tightly to form a fist. Thrust them out again and again pull them in. Keep repeating this, pushing the fingers out hard and pulling them in equally hard. This strengthens not only the fingers but also the forearms. It is a very good general-purpose exercise. Anything between 50 and 200 stretches become fairly painful, hard work for all but the extremely strong player.

Arm circles

To strengthen the arms, hold them out to the side at shoulder height and start by simply turning the arms and hands to form small circles, perhaps six inches in diameter. Gradually extend this to form larger circles, going on and on with the exercise until it becomes punishing in the arms. This can be developed further for the strong player by doing the same holding, say, a 6-iron and 7-iron.

Book lifts

A wrist exercise for the club golfer is to hold a fairly large book, say three inches thick, between the fingers and thumbs of both hands.

Hold the arms out at full stretch and simply hinge the wrists up and back, with the book firmly in place. This can be built up both in the size and thickness of the book used and in the number of lifts completed.

*** Squeezing a squash ball

A general hand exercise which is very useful for keeping the fingers supple and strong is to squeeze a squash ball between the fingers, just working it around in the palm of the hand, pressing hard with the fingertips. In this way the fingers are kept mobile and supple.

*** Winding up a weight

Use a short pole, say two feet six inches in length, such as a broken broom handle, and tie to the centre of this on a piece of string approximately four feet long a weighted object, ideally something like a small paint can with a handle, which will balance and which can be filled with weighted objects. Hold your arms out at full stretch in front of you, supporting the pole with the hands held above it. Now wind the string up on the pole by twisting it in your hands until the weight is lifted off the floor and reaches the pole. This is a simple exercise and one of the most strengthening of all for the forearms. It can be made progressively more difficult as strength develops.

Using Dumbbells

The aspiring top-class player will derive a great deal from weight training, particularly in building up strength in the arms and wrists. Weight training should generally be done with very careful supervision but these four exercises are simple enough to do, and great favourites among professional golfers. The weights used should feel to be perhaps 60 to 70 per cent of the maximum load possible. Emphasis is put on training and not lifting.

Wrist twists – unsupported

Hold the dumbbells with your elbows firmly against your sides and turn the forearms out to the sides and then inwards, over and back, over and back, with as much movement as possible. This encourages flexibility in the wrists and is a strengthening exercise particularly for the upper arms.

Wrist twists – supported

Hold the weight in one hand with the elbow supported on the edge of a table. Twist the wrist and forearm from side to side, through as much movement as possible, building up flexibility and also strengthening the forearms.

Forearm lifts

Hold the weights in front of you, both elbows tucked into the sides, palms of the hands facing you. Hinge the weights up and down towards you and back, developing and strengthening the whole arm.

Arm lifts

Hang your arms down to your sides with a weight in each hand, palms facing inwards. Now lift the arms into a horizontal position and return them to the side slowly. This develops and strengthens the whole arm to the shoulders.

Leg Exercises

Sitting against a wall

One of the finest exercises for strengthening the thigh muscles is to adopt a sitting position, back against a wall, knees forming an approximate right angle. The position can usually only be held at first for a minute or so before the upper legs begin to feel the work involved. A well-known skiing exercise which is just as applicable to the golfer.

Touching the toes

This exercise keeps the hamstrings loose and is a general toning up exercise for the backs of the legs. Correctly the exercise should *not* involve a bouncing movement but should purely be a case of easing the finger tips further down towards the ground. For those to whom this is simple, an adaptation is to stand on a step and feel the fingers stretched down beyond floor level.

★★★ Leg presses

Stand with the left foot on a firm chair or stool and push up on this leg until the leg is straight. Then lower yourself *slowly* to the floor again,

Supported wrist twists

landing gently on the right foot. Push up with the left leg again and back down again. Repeat this initially 20 times with the left leg, 20 with the right – an excellent leg strengthening exercise for the good golfer – gradually building up the number of presses.

Leg lifts

Sit on the floor, hands behind you, and slowly raise both legs, keeping them completely straight. Lower them slowly and keep repeating this until the benefit is felt.

★★★ Ball bag lifts

Sit on the edge of a high table, a practice ball bag of 30 golf balls hooked over your right foot. Lift the ball bag off the ground until your right leg straightens as near horizontally as possible. Repeat this until you feel the leg working hard, increasing the weight load and the number of lifts as the legs strengthen. Repeat with left leg as above.

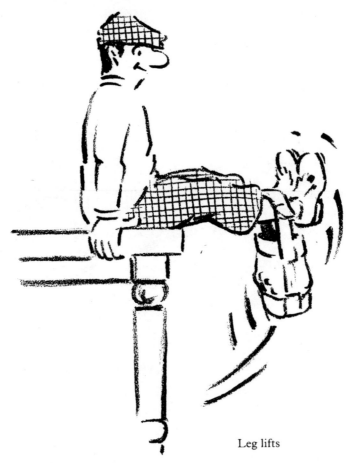

Leg lifts

Ankle twists

Good golf requires looseness and freedom in the feet and ankles, in particular in the left ankle to enable the body to turn through to the target at the finish. Stand with the feet apart the width of the shoulders, feet pointing straight ahead, holding the back of a chair at arm's length and as high as possible. Keeping the arms and shoulder virtually motionless twist the hips to the left and then to the right, preferably until the hips can easily move to be at right angles to the left foot.

Inverted leg lifts

Lie on your front, hands clasping the back of your neck. Now lift the legs and head slowly, just a few inches off the ground. This is a general strengthening exercise for the legs, abdomen and back – but very definitely not for anyone with the slightest back problem.

General Fitness

Running on the spot

For those who don't see themselves jogging or cycling round the streets, running on the spot is a good alternative. This can be done at your own pace for extended periods and gives an excellent way to improve all-round fitness without making a spectacle of yourself or encountering problems with inclement weather.

Skipping

Even better than running on the spot is a pro-gramme of skipping, preferably pulling the knees well up to the chest and bouncing nimbly on the balls of the feet.

Cycling and swimming

These are both excellent activities for the golfer from a general fitness point of view, with the proviso that swimming must be very much an off-season sport and definitely not within a week or so before tournaments.

*** Sergeant jumps

Stand beside a wall, right side to the wall. Stretch upwards with the right arm and fingers to judge the highest spot you can reach from this position. Put a chalk mark on the wall 12 inches above this. Now resume your original position and jump to touch the chalk mark, then bend down to touch the floor. Start with 20 with the right, 20 with the left, adjusting the chalk mark up or down according to your own spring, but giving a target which is realistic but quite hard to achieve.

Shuttle runs

This is an exercise for the practice ground or garden. Set down two golf clubs 20 yards apart and run from one to the other, putting a hand down beyond the club at either end. Keep repeating this, accelerating hard, stopping and turning.

Step-throughs

This is a seemingly innocuous exercise which is harder than it sounds. Grasp both ends of a club – say a 6-iron – and step between your arms and the club, first over with the right foot and leg, and then over and through with the left. Once through, club behind you, step back over the club again. This requires agility and suppleness in the body, arms and legs.

Step-throughs

*** Running with the club

Running on the spot, jogging and skipping are all good exercises for general fitness. The work rate can be increased tremendously by running holding a club in both hands above the head. An excellent exercise is to run at speed, club held in front of you and then to raise the arms and club above the head, continuing to run at the same speed for as long as possible. Then lower the arms and continue jogging until you feel you can hold the club overhead again. Either try this in the confines of a squash court or gym, or use it as an alternative to ordinary running on the spot.

Lastly: having hit all the practice balls up the practice ground, collect them, running and bounding as fast as possible to complete the practice session.